Clarifying the Great Commission

Jesus' Parting Gifts to His Church

Daniel Christian Voth

CONCORDIA PUBLISHING HOUSE · SAINT LOUIS

To my wife, Crystal,
who encouraged me
to write and occupied the kids while I did so;
to my parents, who brought me up in The Faith;
and to the teachers, instructors,
and mentors who urged me
to dig through the Scriptures,
for they are able to make one wise
unto salvation in Christ Jesus, our Lord.

Published by Concordia Publishing House
3558 S. Jefferson Ave., St. Louis, MO 63118-3968
1-800-325-3040 · cph.org

1 2 3 4 5 6 7 8 9 10 34 33 32 31 30 29 28 27 26 25

Clarifying the Great Commission
by Daniel C. Voth

For entirely too long, the church has tried to squeeze the Bible into the Great Commission. What if we inverted that and instead used the Scriptures to get at the meaning of what we call the Great Commission? What if instead of laying a procrustean bed of assumptions about how "we need to get out there and witness because people are going to hell!" we instead heard the Great Commission in light of Matthew's Gospel particularly and then the Scriptures as a whole? Well, a delightfully different framework comes into view, and *that* is what Rev. Voth so soundly delivers in this monograph. I cannot recommend this book highly enough to those who love the Word, for here a servant of the Word has provided great insight into a passage that has so often been misused as a cudgel to squelch the joy of life in Christ. Give it a read! You will *not* regret it!

— William Weedon, assistant pastor, St. Paul Lutheran Church, Hamel, Illinois; catechist on Lutheran Public Radio's podcast, *The Word of the Lord Endures Forever*

From promise to command. Clarity to confusion. Certainty to doubt. Building one another up to tearing one another down. Comfort and joy to guilt and shame. A work of God to a work of man. When reading and understanding the Great Commission, American Christianity has lost something quite profound. We have lost the power of Christ and the fullness of His Gospel. With remarkable brevity, clarity, wit, and faithfulness to God's Word, Rev. Daniel Voth reveals the promises and gifts Jesus gives us in His farewell discourse. When you rightly see the Great Commission as God's promise to create, sustain, strengthen, and abide with His church until the end of the age rather than as a command to tell others about Jesus or the church will die, you, too, will be comforted by the Gospel, strengthened in the faith, and enlivened to tell others to "come and see."

— Rev. Dr. Adam Filipek, pastor of Holy Cross Lutheran Church and Immanuel Lutheran Church, Lidgerwood, North Dakota; adjunct professor of practical theology, Concordia Seminary, St. Louis; author of *Life in Christ: Rooted, Woven, and Grafted into God's Story*

Contents

Now the eleven disciples went to Galilee, to the mountain to which Jesus had directed them. And when they saw Him they worshiped Him, but some doubted. And Jesus came and said to them, "All authority in heaven and on earth has been given to Me. Go therefore and make disciples of all nations, baptizing them in the name of the Father and of the Son and of the Holy Spirit, teaching them to observe all that I have commanded you. And behold, I am with you always, to the end of the age."

Matthew 28:16–20

Introduction

The Great Commission. It has become a hallmark of American Christianity. You can hardly attend a church service or Bible study or conference without hearing the speaker or leader mention the Great Commission. This charge to Christians is recorded in the last verses of the Holy Gospel according to Matthew and comes directly from the lips of the Lord Jesus Christ. With this heading comes a set of assumptions that are widely held by the Christian Church in America (from my experience, the church body or organization doesn't matter) and likely across the globe. Verses 19–20 are trumpeted as the marching orders for the church on earth and are adopted by many congregations and church bodies as the mission statement that every Christian must obey. These verses are dogmatically held with such compassion, vigor, and tenacity that one can almost surmise that if Christians do not actively participate in the mandate, the church will cease to exist. Or, if it doesn't end, it will not have the prominent role it had in days gone by—and it must be recovered so that the world will have some sort of hope.

If we listen to the chatter of the modern church in America, we may get a great sense that the church is dying and in jeopardy of disappearing altogether if we don't get more people to join our congregations. (I say a bit more about that mentality in just a while.) Many have turned to the Great Commission as motivation and have demanded that every Christian must obey these words, because if we don't, no one else will. It's as if Jesus' final words to His disciples according to Matthew mean "You have to go—anywhere, everywhere, all the time—and make disciples for Jesus. If you don't, no one will, and those people will end up in hell because you did not listen to Jesus. You have to use any and every means necessary to win nonbelievers for Jesus."

I realize that this is a harsh and cynical restating of the Great Commission, but I have heard it preached and taught this way too often. This sort of teaching leads to a pathetic, uninspiring, unbiblical picture of Jesus. It tells people that even though He healed the sick, made people who were paralyzed walk, and raised the dead, He cannot make disciples or build and sustain His church without us.

I sincerely believe that this is not what people intend to convey. But when we follow the standard presentation of the Great Commission as stated in the previous paragraph, this is what we end up with—a less than divine Jesus. There appears to be some great omissions to the Great Commission that we need to explore.

Origins of the Term *the Great Commission*

The term *the Great Commission* refers to Matthew 28:19–20:

> Go therefore and make disciples of all nations, baptizing them in the name of the Father and of the Son and of the Holy Spirit, teaching them to observe all that I have commanded you. And behold, I am with you always, to the end of the age.

If you simply say "the Great Commission," this is what most modern Christians think you are referring to. They may also assume that this label has been used throughout the history of the Christian Church. That would not be correct.

> It turns out that this passage may have got its summary label from a Dutch missionary Justinian von Welz (1621–88), but it was Hudson Taylor, nearly two hundred years later, who popularized the use of "The Great Commission." So, it seems like Welz or some other Post-Reformation missionary probably coined the term "The Great Commission" and since that time, the passage has been the theme for countless mission talks and conferences.[1]

No one is 100 percent certain where the label originated. You can find countless guesses on the internet, but none state definitively who first uttered those words. That said, no matter where the label originated, it is a modern expression in the

1 Robbie F. Castleman, "The Last Word: The Great Commission: Ecclesiology," *Themelios: An International Journal for Students of Theological and Religious Studies* 32, no. 3 (2007): 68.

two-thousand-year history of the New Testament. We have only referred to these verses as the Great Commission in the last two to four centuries. The term is not found in Scripture, except in the headings that have been added by publishers. This lack of historical evidence for the use of this title should be the first clue that perhaps something is amiss when it comes to this term and how we have understood what it supposedly means.

Here's a quick word on missing terms or titles in the Bible. You won't find the phrase "the Great Commission," but you also don't find "the Ten Commandments" in many Bible translations, except in headings added by publishers. They are referred to literally as "the ten words" in Exodus 34:28 and Deuteronomy 4:13; 10:4. Most modern translations use the term *commandments* for the Hebrew word *words* for clarity since that is how we commonly refer to them. You also won't find the word *Trinity*, which we can see clearly taught throughout the Bible, including in Genesis 1:1–3; Numbers 6:22–27; Isaiah 6:3; Matthew 3:16–17; 28:19; Luke 1:35; 3:21–22; and 2 Corinthians 13:14, to cite some. The church has adopted words to express ideas that are clearly taught in the Scriptures. Just because a term or title is not found in the revealed Scriptures and is used by the church does not mean it is wrong or misguided. The use of common terms assists the church with a common language when all agree to their definitions. Although the term *the Great Commission* has become as accepted and used as much as many other terms, it is still new in the church's history and may cause

Christians to gloss over some very important and clear teachings from Matthew 28 that should not be ignored.

Let's look at a few examples of how the Great Commission is understood in the modern Christian context.

Modern Uses of *the Great Commission*[*]

In a best-selling book published in the 1990s about a church's purpose or what it is committed to, author Rick Warren came up with the slogan "A Great Commitment to the Great Commandment and the Great Commission will grow a Great Church."[2] That's a lot of "greats"! You can hear the elements of what you must do in this understanding of the responsibility of every Christian. You, as a Christian, must belong to a church that places your greatest efforts, along with those of everyone else who belongs to that church, on obeying the greatest commandment, which is to love God with all you have and your neighbor in the same way, while also carrying out the greatest mandate to make more people like you so that you can be part of a great (understand that this "great" is purely about numbers, not quality) group of people gathered on Sunday mornings.

Author Mark Mittelberg states, "Jesus gave us a universal mission statement in the Great Commission, and any church that neglects any aspect of it—including the 'making disciples' part—is disregarding his divine mandate. What about your church or ministry? Is your

* See also Lucas Woodford's review of the literature that advocates this understanding of the Great Commission in *Great Commission, Great Confusion, or Great Confession?: The Mission of the Holy Christian Church* (Wipf & Stock, 2012), 54–58.

2 Rick Warren, *The Purpose Driven Church: Every Church Is Big in God's Eyes* (Zondervan, 1995), 103.

mission clear? Is it aligned with the Great Commission?"[3] That statement is very heavy-handed—sort of like Jesus was giving one last law to His disciples that we must obey in order to get into heaven.

I enjoy this next one. Although "the Great Commission" is not used in the Scriptures, that didn't stop one author from saying this: "It is a sin to be good if God has called us to be great. Christians refer to Matthew 28:18–20 as the Great Commission, not the Good Commission."[4] Christians use the word *great* with these verses, but Jesus did not.

Again, according to the contemporary Christian understanding, the final verses of Matthew's Gospel are a command that Christians must carry out lest the church die and cease to exist. I have even seen and heard presentations that place a huge burden of guilt on people. They state that if we are not going on mission trips, not standing in the parking lots of local big box stores seeking to win people for Jesus, and not constantly talking about Jesus to strangers, then we are not fulfilling the Great Commission, and people will go to hell on account of our failure to do so. The Great Commission has sort of become a huge two-by-four to clobber people over the head with. It falsely places people's eternal salvation in question if they have not gone out and made disciples for Jesus.

This cannot be the heart of Jesus' final words to His disciples as recorded in Matthew!

---

3 Mark Mittelberg, *Building a Contagious Church: Revolutionizing the Way We View and Do Evangelism* (Zondervan, 2002), 25–26.

4 Thom S. Rainer, *Breakout Churches: Discover How to Make the Leap* (Zondervan, 2005), 15.

Unintended Consequences

An unintended or unintentional consequence of the modern understanding of the Great Commission is a change in approach to the edification of the saints—those who already know and confess Jesus as Lord and Savior. A result of so much emphasis on recruiting people to the local congregation is that those who already believe in Jesus tend to be marginalized in their faith, edification, and growth. When the thought process in the modern church focuses on what we must do, what Christ has done for us is minimized or, worse, omitted.

In many congregations, the emphasis has shifted from preaching what Jesus has done for us by His life, death, and resurrection to how we must go beyond the doors and evangelize, recruit, bring in, and make people become Christians. Justification for this shift is rationalized with statements about how the church's membership is declining year after year, how the church is in jeopardy of dying and disappearing altogether unless we get more people to join our congregations. This has led to a strange approach to Sunday mornings. The rationale goes along these lines: Those who are not coming and those who don't believe in Jesus as their Lord and Savior will not walk in our doors unless we make it comfortable for them. We need to conduct a survey of our neighborhood or community to see what people want from a church, what needs the average non-churchgoing, non-Christian person wants or needs the local congregation to do and be. Based on the results of this survey, the church will change its worship style, avoid churchy language and feel, and ditch anything that looks or smells like the church of old in an attempt to lure people to attend and thereby boost attendance.

The unintentional consequence is a church that asks those who do not already come to church what those who do come should change in the hopes that those who don't come will suddenly come. In other words, the people who already attend church regularly are required to get rid of traditions, doctrines, and practices to make those who don't attend church feel comfortable. This marketing strategy is not found in the Scriptures.

Think of it this way. Pandas only eat bamboo. It would be unwise for the pandas to give up bamboo in the hopes that the tigers would come join them and become pandas. This would result in death for the pandas. I find it strange that there are people who think that if the church gives up her heritage, doctrines, traditions, and liturgies, non-Christians will flock into her buildings. Giving up the traditions of the church to align with society starves the faithful. Omitting the traditional hymns (so rich with the Gospel), opening Holy Communion to anyone in attendance, and leaving sin out of sermons turns the Divine Service into an hour of entertainment instead of a time when Christ Jesus is present with us in the Word and Sacraments. Yet this is the strategy churches all across the globe have used for the last forty to fifty years.

Please don't get me wrong. We need to tell people about Jesus, the only begotten Son of God, who came to forgive our sins and give us eternal life by His crucifixion, death, burial, and resurrection. There are plenty of places in Scripture outside of the last five verses of Matthew's Gospel that make clear the exhortation to tell people about Jesus as Lord and Savior. There are better examples in Matthew's Gospel of how and why Christians should point people to Jesus, with implications for our life together as His brothers and sisters. (We will consider these examples later.) The way we have been led to believe that Christ demands everyone to be a parking lot missionary is not what Christ was saying to His disciples at the end of Matthew 28. There is more than meets the eye in this passage, especially eyes that have been instructed for generations that this is the only way to read it.

Historical Use of Matthew 28:16–20

Prior to the seventeenth century, the church viewed the final verses of Matthew's Gospel not as the directive for preaching and teaching missions but as the main text for instruction on Baptism from Christ's mouth. Less emphasis was placed on "Go therefore and make disciples" and more on "Baptizing them in the name the Father and of the Son and of the Holy Spirit."

These verses clearly reveal God to be triune—Father, Son, and Holy Spirit. He is one God in three distinct persons, which is most clearly confessed in the Athanasian Creed. Christ also gave us the words we use during the Rite of Holy Baptism in these verses (see Matthew 28:19). Ever since Christ uttered those words, the church has understood His instructions to us. We are to baptize all nations in His name, according to His instructions. We don't make up what we say, as if saying, "I splash water on you in the name of the Creator God, the Redeemer God, and the Sanctifying God," would be following Jesus' instructions. Yes, baptizing can include splashing water. Yes, we refer to the Father as the Creator, the Son as the Redeemer, and the Holy Spirit as the one who sanctifies us. But that phrase is not part of Jesus' command. He clearly instructs us how to carry out Holy Baptism according to His command and instructions, even giving us the very words we should speak.

Liturgical Use of Matthew 28:16–20

Matthew 28:16–20 only appears once in the appointed readings for the Church Year lectionary. It is the appointed Holy Gospel for Holy Trinity Sunday in the Three-Year Lectionary, Year A. As you can quickly deduce from that information, the church connects Jesus' farewell discourse not with a mission festival or mission emphasis but with the celebration of and teaching on the triune God. (In case you're wondering, the lectionary Gospel reading suggestion for a mission observance is Luke 24:44–53, Jesus' final words to His disciples in Luke's account along the Sea of Galilee.)

It is the Gospel text that gives shape and substance to the theme of each Sunday, and Holy Trinity Sunday is no exception. The final discourse in Matthew 28 is the clearest teaching in the Holy Scriptures on the nature of God as three distinct persons in one divine being. Thus, when the church celebrates the nature of God, she turns to these verses. Even the Collect of the Day for Holy Trinity, Year A, echoes our Lord's words:

> Almighty and everlasting God, You have given us grace to acknowledge the glory of the eternal *Trinity* by the *confession* of a true faith and *to worship* the Unity in the power of the Divine Majesty. *Keep us steadfast* in this faith and defend us from all adversities. (*LSB Propers of the Day,* Collect for Holy Trinity A, emphasis added)

As you read this book, these emphases will become more clear. The disciples' first action when they saw the risen Jesus was to worship (see Matthew 28:17). The words of Matthew 28:19 are connected liturgically to Baptism and the triune Godhead—Father, Son, and Holy Spirit—not missions. The confession of a true faith and to be kept steadfast in the faith is the emphasis of Matthew 28:20.

So what are we missing in Jesus' final discourse? Let's see what the following chapters reveal about the Great Commission.

DISCUSSION QUESTIONS

1. What assumptions about the Great Commission are generally held by the Christian Church, particularly in the United States?

2. How do these assumptions line up with what you have heard preached and taught in your church?

3. What are the consequences of these assumptions?

4. How do comments like "God has called us to be great" make you feel about your own walk as a Christian?

5. What changes have you observed in your church or the church in general based on this call to obey the Great Commission?

6. What was the focus of the traditional understanding of Matthew 28:16–20 in the church?

CHAPTER 1

CONTEXT, CONTEXT, CONTEXT

Every realtor knows, as do most people who have ever tried to sell their house, that the most important thing when selling a home is location, location, location. The location of the house, the neighborhood around it, and the community that neighborhood is in matter. The same is true when studying the Holy Scriptures. The location of the passage and the surrounding passages matter to our understanding. When you cite a passage of Scripture apart from its context, you can make the Bible say just about anything you want it to say. Many false teachers have done this and have led people astray. For instance, this verse sounds appropriate for the life of a Christian: “All these I will give you, if you will fall down and worship me” (Matthew 4:9). If you do not know the context of this quote in the Scriptures, it might sound like prosperity preaching: the belief that if you put Jesus first in your life and worship Him with your tithes and offerings, Jesus will give you whatever you want, including all your wildest dreams and wishes. This would be an amazing promise to find in the Scriptures, especially coming from Jesus, but there is one major problem. When you read this verse in context, you learn that these words came from the lips of Satan as he tempted Jesus in the wilderness. Context to a Christian who is reading the Bible is more important than location to someone who is selling a house.

A close friend of mine recounts in his first book an encounter with a New Testament college professor who stated the importance of context in this manner: "A Bible text without a context is a pretext for a prooftext."[5] Proof texting is taking a passage of Scripture out of its context to prove a point. The danger is misunderstanding or even misconstruing what God reveals to us in His Word. One of the key rules for interpreting God's Word is to let Scripture interpret Scripture. This means that theologians, pastors, and anyone else who reads the Bible must let the clear passages of Scripture inform the less clear passages.

Additionally, the Bible cannot contradict itself on any point, so if you think you've found one text that opposes another, just keep reading. This hermeneutic (the rule of biblical interpretation) helps us keep what God has actually said in His Word in check. We read the Bible to understand what God reveals to us and not what we want to reveal to God. His Word stands over our reason and intellect (the ministerial use), not the other way around, where God must conform to our reason and intellect (the magisterial use). We need to let the fullness of the Holy

5 Dan Suelzle, *Misquoted: Rethinking Commonly Misused Bible Verses* (Harvest House Publishers, 2019), 10.

Scriptures interpret the passage we are examining, especially its context within the totality of the Scriptures.

So, if we are going to talk about the final verses of Matthew's Gospel, we need to look at the context so we do not make the verses say something they were not meant to say.

A Simple Approach to Understanding Context

When discussing context, I like to think of an upside-down triangle. This triangle is wide at the top and narrows as you work your way down. Therefore, when discussing biblical context, we start very wide to see how the passage fits within the broad narrative of the divine story of redemption. Then we work our way down, narrowing the context as we go, until we

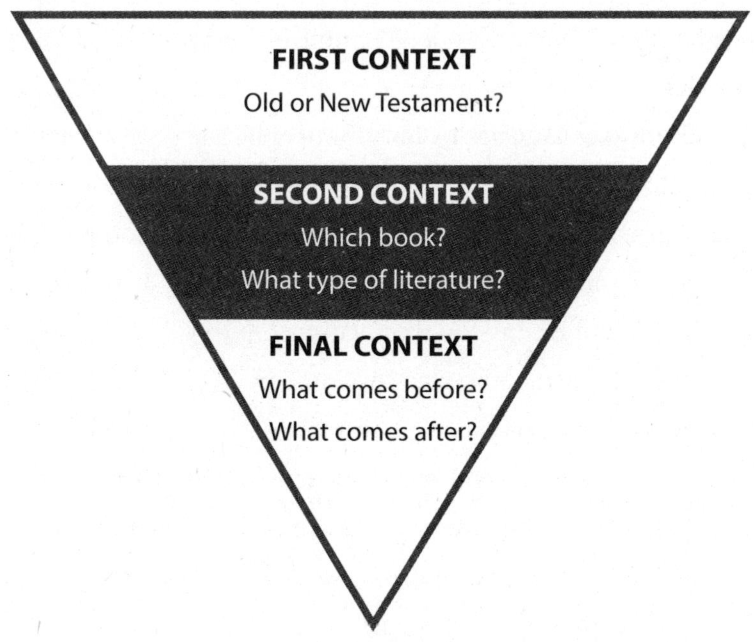

arrive at the bottom, the narrowest context immediately surrounding the passage.

I start by looking at where the passage is located: Old or New Testament. This may seem too basic, but where the passage is located in the Bible gives us critical information. In the Old Testament, we read about people, places, and events that looked forward to the coming of the Christ, the Savior promised to Adam and Eve in Genesis 3. The Gospel accounts of Matthew, Mark, Luke, and John discuss the life and work of Christ Jesus. The remainder of the New Testament is primarily encouragement for Christians to look to Christ, who has come and promises to come again.

Then I look at the book of the Bible where the passage is located. Some biblical books recount history and tell a linear story, like Genesis, Exodus, or Acts. Some books are poetic and use picturesque language to describe people, places, or events. It's helpful to know and understand that when Solomon describes a woman with analogies from nature in Song of Solomon, he is complimenting her (not saying she looks like a deer in the crosshairs) and discussing the relationship of the Bridegroom, Christ, to His Bride, the church. Some books, like Daniel and Revelation, include visions in which images shift and change (like in our dreams). We should avoid reading them literally word for word. Rather, these books are to be understood within the full context of the Scriptures, letting clearer passages inform the less clear passages, as noted above.

The final context I consider is what is happening immediately before and after the passage being discussed. Who has said what and how have the other people reacted? Is there a connection to what just happened? Has the author switched gears? Are there parallel passages in another book of the Bible that can help us understand the context and meaning? These sorts of questions help us see clearly what God is saying in His Word. So here we go.

The Context for Our Discussion

The verses we are examining are in the New Testament, specifically the Gospel according to Matthew. This location tells us we are discussing the visible life and ministry of Jesus Christ from approximately 2 BC to AD 33.[6] Most scholars say that Matthew, one of Jesus' disciples, was writing to a primarily Jewish audience. This is based on the number of times Matthew cites the words and actions of Jesus in fulfillment of the Old Testament, the Jewish prophecies. (This will become more important as we take a closer look at the context of the passage.) This is the broad top of our inverted triangle—the placing of the verses in their proper setting. Let's continue to narrow down our context.

Matthew begins his Gospel account with an efficient way to tell history in a quick fashion—a genealogy. Matthew reminds us that Abraham, the father of the Jewish nation, and David, the greatest king of Israel by which all other kings are measured,

6 For a more detailed account of these dates, see Andrew E. Steinmann, *From Abraham to Paul: A Biblical Chronology*, second edition (Concordia Publishing House, 2024), 206, 248–49.

are part of the lineage of Jesus. This establishes that Jesus has a good pedigree from a human viewpoint, especially to his Jewish readership. Their lineage was critical because they needed to prove their connection to Abraham and the covenant people to whom the promises of God were given. Matthew highlights a few problems in the line, namely the inclusion of Gentiles like Tamar, Rahab, Ruth, and "the wife of Uriah," yet this is done with purpose (see Matthew 1:3, 5, 6).

Next, we come to the birth narrative of Jesus. Matthew doesn't give all the pageantry details that are present in Luke's account, but there are a few things worth noting. First, there was a virgin named Mary who was to marry Joseph. When the Second Person of the Holy Trinity became incarnate and took up residence in the ark of Mary's womb, her betrothed was angry at the situation. "But as he considered these things," the Lord revealed in a vision to Joseph that Mary had committed no sin, that he should continue with his plans to take Mary as his wife, that he was to name the child Jesus, and that all of this was in fulfillment of the prophecies of Isaiah.[7] As part of the fulfillment of the prophet Isaiah's words, the child was going to be "'Immanuel,' (which means, God with us)" (Matthew 1:23). Because we know the end of the story, we can see the first bookend of the Gospel—that Jesus is "God with us"—and the second bookend—that He is with us always to the very end of the age. We'll return to this later.

7 Kenneth E. Bailey, *Jesus Through Middle Eastern Eyes: Cultural Studies in the Gospels* (IVP Academic, 2008), 46.

Take a closer look at Matthew 10 to see the context of our primary verses:

> And He called to Him His twelve disciples and gave them authority over unclean spirits, to cast them out, and to heal every disease and every affliction. . . .
>
> These twelve Jesus sent out, instructing them, "Go nowhere among the Gentiles and enter no town of the Samaritans, but go rather to the lost sheep of the house of Israel. And proclaim as you go, saying, 'The kingdom of heaven is at hand.' Heal the sick, raise the dead, cleanse lepers, cast out demons." (Matthew 10:1, 5–8)

Since we know where we are going, we can see why we stopped at these verses. Jesus gave His disciples authority—a word that is repeated at the end of Matthew. The authority He spoke of in verse 1 and clarified in verse 8 is to drive out demons. In other words, He gave them the power to perform exorcisms and heal people who were sick, including raising the deceased back to life. Notice that this was not any and every authority; it was limited in scope. Christ's words established the scope and set boundaries as to what they were to do and how they were to accomplish the task.

So, too, was the mission given at the end of Matthew 28. Jesus set very clear boundaries regarding the disciples carrying out this authority. They could not go wherever they wanted, blown by the wind on some enlightenment-seeking journey. The disciples were to go only to the Jews. They were not to go to the Gentiles, which Jesus clarified included the Samaritans. We also see that part of their God-given mandate included a command to publicly preach, which is what Jesus was doing (see Matthew 9:35). Here we can see a foreshadowing of what will come after Christ's resurrection.

Matthew 15 reinforces this. Jesus and His disciples traveled far north into the district of Tyre and Sidon. A woman whose daughter was possessed by a demon approached Jesus, begged for His help, and received what seemed like an unloving brush off from Him. After some banter, Jesus finally gave in to her request and sent her away, knowing her daughter was instantly saved.

Matthew records something different compared to Mark's account. In Mark's Gospel, the women is said to be "a Gentile, a Syrophoenician by birth" (Mark 7:26). Matthew digs into the history of the Jews and the constant thorn in the side of Israel, the Canaanites. This woman was not just Gentile but a descendant of people that God had commanded to be completely wiped off the face of the earth. It might surprise you that God commanded a people group to be destroyed. Let's go to Deuteronomy 7 to explore this.

Moses is addressing the children of Israel prior to entering the Promised Land and says,

> When the Lord your God brings you into the land that you are entering to take possession of it, and

> clears away many nations before you, the Hittites, the Girgashites, the Amorites, the *Canaanites*, the Perizzites, the Hivites, and the Jebusites, seven nations more numerous and mightier than you, and when the Lord your God gives them over to you, and you defeat them, then *you must devote them to complete destruction*. You shall make no covenant with them and show no mercy to them. You shall not intermarry with them, giving your daughters to their sons or taking their daughters for your sons, for they would turn away your sons from following Me, to serve other gods. Then the anger of the Lord would be kindled against you, and He would destroy you quickly. But thus shall you deal with them: you shall break down their altars and dash in pieces their pillars and chop down their Asherim and burn their carved images with fire. (Deuteronomy 7:1–5, emphasis added)

Matthew and his Jewish readers would have remembered well that God had commanded their ancestors through Moses not to allow Canaanites or anyone from the other six nations—every one of them Gentile—to be left alive. This command was given to protect the children of Israel from exposure to idolatry. The book of Judges reveals that the children of Israel did not obey this command. From the time of the judges to the Babylonian exile, the history of the Israelites is rife with the consequences of the people's failure to heed God's word.

So, in Matthew 15:21–28, it was a woman not of the lost sheep of Israel but a hated Gentile, a dog, according to Jesus' own words, who called out to Jesus with Jewish messianic terms. It may be confusing to read about how Jesus treated this woman until we realize that Jesus was drawing the attention of His disciples, who were Jewish, to the unquestioning faith of a Gentile woman. This was an eye-opening event for the disciples, and it served as a bridge for them (and us) from the event in Matthew 10 to the event in Matthew 28. Matthew 10 records that Jesus sent the disciples to the lost sheep of Israel. In Matthew 28, Jesus sent the disciples to the Gentiles, echoing the language used in Matthew 10.

Narrowing in, we are led with Jesus to Jerusalem, to His Passion, where He suffered, died on the cross, was buried, and rose from the dead. Finally, we arrive at the last five verses of Matthew. The context is postresurrection and preascension, a narrow window of forty days. The final words of Jesus recorded in Matthew are worthy words to ponder, reflect upon, and understand.

There's one more piece of context that brings us back to location. At the empty tomb, an angel greeted the women with a message for the disciples: Jesus was going to Galilee, where the disciples would see Him (see Matthew 28:7). As the women left the tomb, Jesus Himself met them and told them to tell the disciples the same thing: "Go and tell My brothers to go to Galilee, and there they will see Me" (Matthew 28:10). Matthew does not record any other postresurrection appearance of Jesus. There

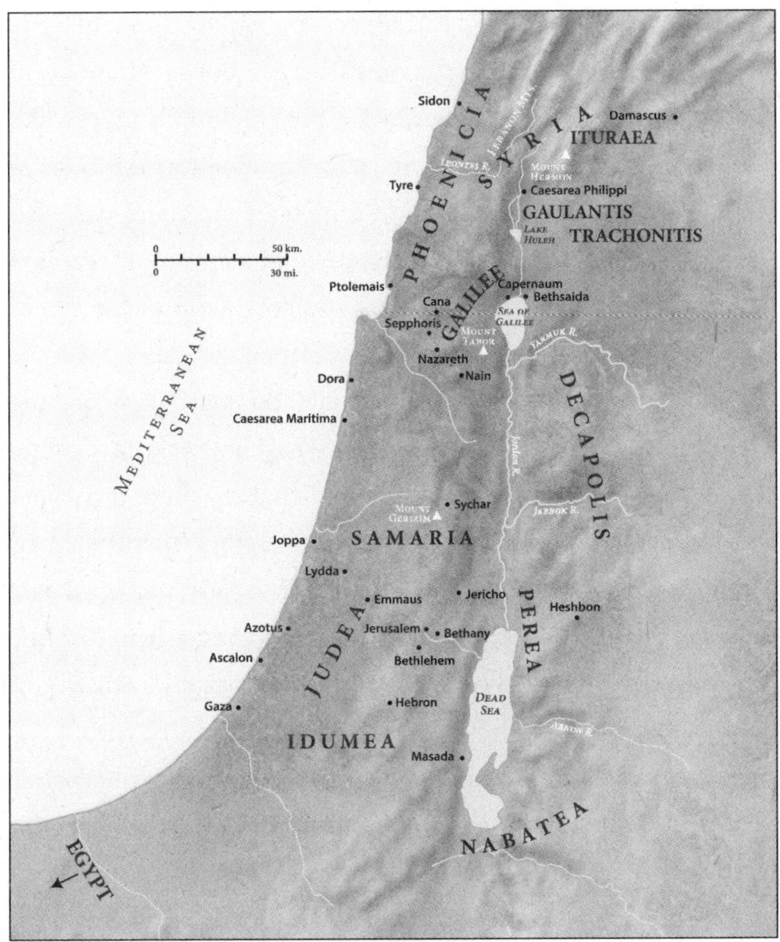

Map © Concordia Publishing House

are no Upper Room appearances like we find in Luke and John, no roadside talk as in Luke, and no morning meal by the Sea of Galilee as in John. The only postresurrection appearance of Jesus with His disciples recorded in Matthew is found in the last five verses of Matthew 28, where they meet Him in Galilee on an unnamed, unidentified mountain.

To get from Jerusalem to Galilee, you had to go north quite a ways. The Sea of Galilee was on its eastern border. There were several towns of importance in Galilee, including places like Nazareth, where Jesus grew up, and Capernaum, the base of Jesus' ministry and the home of Simon Peter. There was also the city of Cana, where Jesus performed His first sign (revealed in John 2:1–12), and Bethsaida on the north end of the Sea of Galilee, a town Jesus and His disciples often visited.

But Galilee did not extend all the way west to the Mediterranean Sea. That area was Syro-Phoenicia, a Gentile region that included Tyre and Sidon. That is where Jesus met the mother of the demon-possessed daughter mentioned in Matthew 15. To the south was Samaria. This land was once part of Israel, but when the Assyrians conquered Samaria in 722 BC, the Assyrians marched off many of the Samarian Israelites and left the poor behind. The Assyrians resettled the area with "people from Babylon, Cuthah, Avva, Hamath, and Sepharvaim" (2 Kings 17:24). These people married the Israelites who were left in Samaria. This created a mixed ethnicity made up of Israelites and Gentiles, known in Jesus' day as Samaritans. According to Jews, they were not among the covenant people. To the south and west was a region known as the Decapolis, literally the "Ten Cities." Jesus went there a few times in His ministry, most notably when He healed the man possessed by a legion of demons. The people who lived there were Gentiles. To the north and west was Gaulantis, a Gentile region as well. One place to note in Gaulantis is the area around Caesarea Philippi, where Peter would make the great confession that Jesus was indeed "the Christ, the Son of the living God" (Matthew 16:16). In other words, although Galilee was populated with Jews, Gentiles lived all around it. This location is part of the context for our discussion.

To summarize, we are in the New Testament Gospel account of Matthew after Jesus' death and resurrection but before His ascension. This account took place in the Jewish land known as Galilee, where Jesus would speak to His disciples for the last time in Matthew 28. This information cannot be omitted. As David J. Bosch wrote, "It is inadmissible to lift these words out of Matthew's Gospel, as it were, allow them a life of their own, and understand them without any reference to the context in which they first appeared. Where this happens, the Great Commission is easily degraded to a mere slogan or used as a pretext for what we in advance decided, perhaps unconsciously, it should mean."[8] In other words, if you lift these verses from their context, you'll have some great omissions, on purpose or by accident.

8 David J. Bosch, *Transforming Mission: Paradigm Shifts in Theology of Mission* (Maryknoll, NY: Orbis Books, 2011), 57.

DISCUSSION QUESTIONS

1. What is proof texting? How have you seen passages of Scripture taken out of context simply to prove someone's false belief?

2. Why does the proper context matter when studying the Bible?

3. Why do we let clear passages of Scripture inform the less clear passages?

4. Describe how the inverted triangle (see p. 21) is a helpful tool for proper biblical interpretation.

5. What boundaries did Jesus set for the disciples' first preaching expedition? How does this differ from what you know and understand about the Great Commission?

6. God's command in Deuteronomy 7 may look harsh and uncharacteristic of God at first, but it is there to protect God's people from actions that will destroy them and their faith. How do the Commandments do the same thing for us today?

7. How does biblical geography help us understand another level of context of the passage?

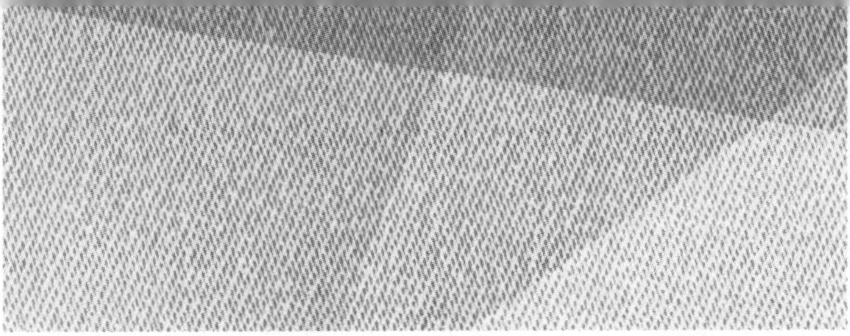

CHAPTER 2

Matthew 28:16

Now the eleven disciples
went to Galilee, to the mountain to
which Jesus had directed them.

Jesus instructed His eleven remaining disciples to a mountain in Galilee after His resurrection. This place was prearranged with them at some point, although the Bible does not tell us when the arrangement was made. This detail is part of the great omission in almost every discussion of the Great Commission. Yet the location of this visit between Jesus and His disciples sets the stage for what follows.

Good Near Eastern Thought Is Not Good English Grammar

English translators strive to remain faithful to the original Greek text as they render God's Word into good English sentence construction. The problem is English does not use phrases the same way Greek does when telling a story. My favorite example of this is in Paul's epistle to the church in Ephesus. In Ephesians 1, Paul writes a great doxology, a song of praise to the triune God that is one long, continuous sentence full of participial phrases in the Greek and spans verses 3–14. According to standard rules of English grammar, that would be a nightmare of a sentence. So those twelve verses are broken into five sentences in the English Standard Version of the Bible. The New International Version breaks those same verses into six sentences. The Evangelical Heritage Edition breaks them into eleven sentences. The use of articles in Greek is more accurate than in English because the language highlights exactly who the subject is, what the object is, and what the action is. This level of specificity is difficult to convey in English. Plus, leaving those verses as one long sentence would sound strange to our modern ears.

It can be helpful at times to have a more literal translation that slows down the reading and follows the structure of the Greek so the reader can get the full nuance of what the author was saying. Additionally, the writers of the Bible employed what Dr. Kenneth Bailey, who taught in and lived in the Middle East for more than forty years, called "Hebrew parallelisms":

> The peoples of the Middle East, ancient and modern, have for millennia constructed poetry and some prose using parallelisms. . . . These parallelisms were put together into what I have chosen to call "prophetic homilies." The building blocks of these homilies are various combinations of the Hebrew parallelisms. Sometimes ideas are presented in pairs that form a straight-line sequence and appear on the page in an AA BB CC pattern. At

> other times, ideas are presented and then repeated backward in an A B CC B A outline. These can be called "inverted parallelism" (they are also named "ring composition" and "chiasm"). A third rhetorical style I refer to as "step parallelism" because the parallelisms follow an ABC ABC pattern. Often these three basic styles are combined in a single homily.[9]

It can be helpful to present the text in a nonparagraph form to better show the parallelisms for those not used to hearing the Hebrew parallelisms. English grammar rules do not like this, but the benefit it brings in allowing us to see the parallels of thought with a text, or "homily," as Dr. Bailey calls them, is well worth breaking those rules. Therefore, throughout the rest of this book, I will use my own translation of Matthew 28:16–20 supplemented with a few others where a more literal translation will be helpful for our discussion. My translations are identified with the credit line "(Voth)." I will also employ the lessons learned from Dr. Bailey and use a format that visually highlights the parallelisms that I believe are in the text.

The first verse we will investigate in my more literal translation reads,

> [16]The eleven disciples journeyed into Galilee
> to the mountain which Jesus
> designated to them,
>
> (Voth)

9 Bailey, *Jesus Through Middle Eastern Eyes*, 13–14.

The scene plays out like this: Following the very strange turn of Jesus' arrest, crucifixion, death, and resurrection, the eleven disciples left Jerusalem after the Feast of the Passover and returned home to Galilee. They gathered on a mountain—at a time and a place told to them by Jesus—where they encountered the risen Lord.

Mountain Encounters in the Old Testament

Meeting with God on a mountain should bring several key biblical events to mind. Perhaps the most famous mountain in all of Scripture is Mount Sinai. The events leading up to and flowing from this theophany comprise four of the five Books of Moses. They are referenced in some fashion in almost every other Old Testament book. *Theophany* is a word for a visible appearance of God to mankind. The appearance of God to Moses on Mount Sinai was a major event in the life of the children of Israel. They spent an entire year at this mountain, as Moses often disappeared into the thick smoke and lightning that resided on the top of the mountain to speak with God.

This was not the first time God had revealed Himself to Moses on this mountain. The first time was when God appeared to Moses in a burning bush. Moses was tending the sheep of his father-in-law, Jethro, when he saw a bush that was burning yet not consumed (see Exodus 3). He went to check out the fire. When you see something burning, it's natural to want to check it out, especially when there is something spectacular about the fire, like the one described in Exodus 3. As Moses approached the fire, the Angel of the Lord spoke from the bush. It is clear that this messenger was the Second Person of the Trinity—the Son of God, the preincarnate Jesus. God the Son called out to Moses with instructions to go back to Egypt, save the children of Israel from their enslavement, and bring them to this very same mountain to worship Him. This is the context for the exodus. God wanted to save His people so that they would receive His gift of salvation. After they were saved from their enemy, Pharaoh and his army, through a watery crossing at the Red Sea (think Baptism, as Paul says in 1 Corinthians 10:1–2, and a foreshadowing of Christ's death and resurrection), they arrived at the mountain God had designated to them via Moses. There, they could worship Him and receive His gifts.

In 1 Kings 19:9–18, we read about another man who went to Mount Sinai to receive gifts from God. After slaughtering the prophets of Baal, the prophet Elijah fled for his life when the angry Queen Jezebel threatened to kill him. He was brought to Sinai (called Mount Horeb in 1 Kings 19) by the Angel of the Lord. There, the Word of the Lord (that is, the preincarnate Word of the Lord that John 1:1 identifies as Jesus) came to Elijah with a gift. In that account, God spoke to Elijah not through a great and mighty windstorm, an earthquake, or a fire, but finally through a small whisper. The Lord revealed to Elijah that He had preserved seven thousand people in Israel who had not worshiped Baal but were faithful to the Lord.

The account of the near sacrifice of Isaac did not take place on Sinai, but we should examine it to understand why Jesus directed His disciples to meet Him on a mountain. Twenty-five years after God promised them an heir, Abraham and Sarah were gifted a son, Isaac, by the Lord. Later, God asked Abraham to journey to the land of Moriah to present his only son as an offering on a mountain He would guide them to. Abraham, Isaac, and two servants made the three-day journey (which should bring to mind the number of days Jesus spent in the tomb) to Mount Moriah. Then Abraham told the servants, "Stay here with the donkey; I and the boy will go over there and worship and come again to you" (Genesis 22:5). It is not clear at first, but notice the future tenses in that verse: we will go, we will worship (that is, receive God's gift), we will return. Abraham knew God had instructed him to sacrifice (that is, kill) his only son Isaac. Still, he told the servants that both of them, he and Isaac, would come back to the servants. That shows Abraham's faith in God's power to resurrect! Abraham and Isaac went up the mountain to the place of sacrifice, with Isaac carrying the wood, most likely on his back, which is what he would have been laying on to be sacrificed. The text even suggests that Isaac believed in resurrection, which is why he willingly submitted to his father when Abraham started tying him up. This only-begotten son of the father went willingly to be sacrificed. Just as it was all about to come to a bloody end for Isaac, the Angel of the Lord called out to stop this sacrifice and provided a substitute, a ram (that is, a male lamb), whose head was encircled in thorns. The ram was sacrificed in Isaac's place. One final thought on this account, which is dripping with Jesus, is that the only-begotten Son of the Father was the willing substitute sacrifice who laid on the wood of the cross, suffered, died, and rose from the dead to forgive our sins and give us eternal life.

We are not told how old Isaac was when this account occurred, but he was obviously old enough to carry a large amount of wood necessary for a burnt sacrifice up a mountain. I think all my Sunday School illustrations showed him as a young teenager. He could have been. The only other date we have for him is in Genesis 23:1, which mentions the death of Sarah. She was one hundred twenty-seven at the time of her death, which means Isaac was thirty-seven. The events on Mount Moriah happened some time before Isaac turned thirty-seven. Think about that. Isaac could have been thirty-three or thirty-four, approximately the same age as Jesus when He was sacrificed on the cross willingly.

Notice the common theme running through these mountain encounters. Each time, the Second Person of the Trinity, the preincarnate Jesus, met these people to give them a gift, an act of divine service to His people. Moses, Elijah, Abraham, and Isaac were served by the Son of God as they received His Word of Law and Gospel, His commands and promises, His death and life. The preincarnate Jesus met with His people on a mountain, a place He Himself designated, to give them His gifts. These accounts help set the context for the end of Matthew's Gospel, when Jesus met with His disciples.

Mountain Encounters in the New Testament

The final mountain we should visit is the Mount of Transfiguration, which we read about in Matthew 17:1–8; Mark

9:2–13; and Luke 9:28–36. One week after Peter confessed that Jesus is the Christ, the Son of the Most High God, Jesus took Peter, James, and John to a high mountain. This mountain could well have been in Galilee, as many presume, and could have been the same mountain where His farewell discourse was spoken. Jesus revealed His full glory at His transfiguration as He visited with Moses and Elijah, a scene calling us back to Mount Sinai. According to Luke, they discussed Jesus' exodus, often translated as "departure," which He was to complete in Jerusalem.

Moses' foreshadowing of Christ cannot be missed when we follow the order of events. The preincarnate Jesus talked with Moses on Mount Sinai in a burning bush (that is, a bush in a bright and dazzling light). Having completed the exodus, Moses was instructed to return with the twelve tribes of Israel to the very same mountain to worship God (that is, to receive His gifts, which He was about to give them). Next, the incarnate Jesus talked with Moses and Elijah on a mountain and was transfigured in a bright and dazzling light. Then, having completed His exodus through death, Christ returned with the disciples, perhaps to the same mountain, and gave them His gifts.

The timing of this meeting between Jesus and His disciples, in accordance with the other Gospels, is after His resurrection and before His ascension (forty days after the resurrection, as recorded in Acts 1). This event likely occurred after many of Jesus' postresurrection appearances recorded in Luke and John. John 21 records that the disciples returned to Galilee. This fits logically in the context, in that the disciples were in the region and journeying to this mountain was geographically feasible.

In any case, we know that Jesus had assembled the disciples on the mountain to give them His parting gifts. As He prepared to ascend to the right hand of His Father and no longer be bodily visible on earth, He called them as God called Israel of old to give them gifts as they prepared to live in the wilderness. Paul captures this well when he writes,

"Ascending on high he led captivity captive;
he gave gifts to men." . . .
And he himself gave some *as* apostles
and some *as* prophets
and some *as* evangelists
and some *as* pastors and teachers
for the equipping of the saints,
for the work of the ministry,
for building up the body of Christ.

(Ephesians 4:8, 11–12 LEB)

Paul understood that Christ Jesus gave specific gifts to His church at His ascension:

> People are freely justified for Christ's sake, through faith, when they believe that they are received into favor and that their sins are forgiven for Christ's sake. By His death, Christ made satisfaction for our sins. God counts this faith for righteousness in His sight (Romans 3 and 4 [3:21–26; 4:5]).

(Augsburg Confession, Article 4, paragraph 2)

The next article in the Augsburg Confession expounds on how this faith is delivered to people:

> So that we may obtain this faith, the ministry of teaching the Gospel and administering the Sacraments was instituted. Through the Word and Sacraments, as through instruments, the Holy Spirit is given [John 20:22]. He works faith, when and where it pleases God [John 3:8], in those who hear the good news that God justifies those who believe that they are received into grace for Christ's sake. (Augsburg Confession, Article 5, paragraphs 1–3)

Often omitted from the discussion of the Great Commission is those who were present. Judas had killed himself, but the remaining eleven disciples were with Jesus on the mountain to receive His gifts. The first gift was the office of the holy ministry, to which God calls men as gifts to proclaim the faith to the church through the Word and Sacraments. This gift was manifested in the Eleven, the apostles and evangelists, then those who would occupy that office after their death. Those who filled the office after the era of the apostles are called "pastor/shepherd" and "teacher" by Paul in the New Testament, including in Ephesians 4:11. These gifts are the instruments through which Christ imparts His other gifts to His church. These other gifts are specifically stated in the rest of Jesus' discourse on that mountain. And the purpose of these gifts is to equip the saints in the true doctrines of Christ as we live in the wilderness in order that we may all be brought safely home to the eternal promised land.

DISCUSSION QUESTIONS

1. What benefits can come from a more literal translation that ignores standard English grammatical rules?

2. Today we speak of "mountaintop experiences" as times of great personal spiritual highs. How does that differ from biblical mountain encounters with God?

3. What is a theophany? Where do we see theophanies in the Scriptures?

4. What common theme is seen in all the mountain encounters mentioned? What role did the preincarnate/incarnate Jesus play in these encounters?

5. What pattern of divine service do we see in these mountaintop accounts? What does this pattern teach us about our daily life?

6. What is the significance of these verses, which were the last words Jesus spoke to His disciples before His ascension?

7. When was the last time you heard this verse discussed as part of the Great Commission? What insight does it bring to the understanding of these verses?

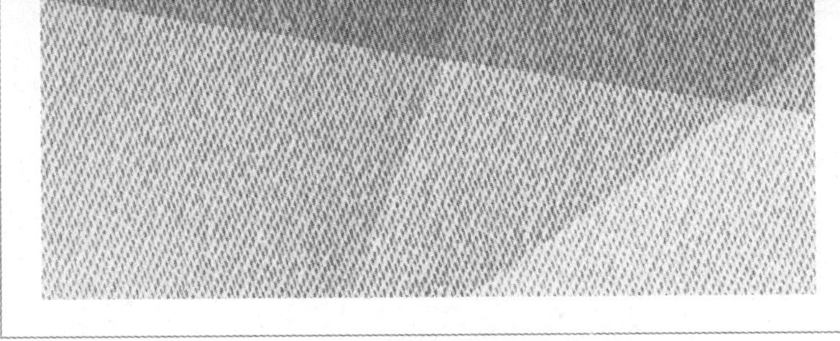

CHAPTER 3

MATTHEW 28:17

And when they saw Him they
worshiped Him, but some doubted.

Verse 17 starts as a continuation of the action that happened on the mountain. The eleven disciples were there when Jesus arrived. When they saw Him, they had two reactions: one physical, one mental. We read,

16The eleven disciples journeyed into Galilee
to the mountain which Jesus
designated to them,
17and having seen Him,
they worshiped,
but some doubted.

(Voth)

The first action is "they worshiped." The Scriptures teach us that worship is not something we do *for* God; it is a response to what God has done for us—our reaction to His love, mercy, and grace. You will recall that when I discussed the mountains and worship in chapter 2 ("Mountain Encounters in the Old Testament" and "Mountain Encounters in the New Testament"), I said that worship is the act of receiving God's gifts.

Receiving Gifts as Worship

American Christianity has turned worship upside down, making worship something we do or will do for God. But in biblical worship, we come to God and assume a stance of humility and declare that He is our God. We show up on Sunday mornings to show God how dedicated we are to Him, that we did not sleep in or stay home to watch our favorite football team or practice casting the fishing rod or swinging the golf club. We join with others to sing our songs to Him. We bring an offering to support the work of our church in our community and maybe toss in a bit extra for the not-yet-Christian people in Africa. We say, "It's all about You, Jesus."

But in the American context, it's really all about us. We have turned worship on its head from God giving us gifts to us doing something, lots of things, everything, for God. Remember in the introduction when I said some speakers give the impression that Jesus needs us to build and sustain His church? That idea applies here. They try to convince us that Jesus needs us to worship Him with our love songs in church.

But that is not worship in a biblical sense. When the children of Israel went to Mount Sinai to worship God, it wasn't their idea. God instructed Moses to bring the people to Him at that designated place to receive His gifts, which included the Ten

Commandments, the tabernacle, the ark of the covenant, and all the appointments for offering sacrifices to cover their sins.

It was not Abraham's idea to offer up his only-begotten son as a sacrifice. God called Abraham and showed him the place where he and Isaac were to worship Him—that is, to receive the gift of a substitute sacrifice, foreshadowing what Christ Jesus would do for us.

Think back further to the Garden of Eden. Once God had created man, He gave him His word: "You may surely eat of every tree of the garden, but of the tree of the knowledge of good and evil you shall not eat, for in the day that you eat of it you shall surely die" (Genesis 2:16–17). This was God's gift to man: a place to worship Him by listening to His Word. Then God created woman (see Genesis 2:22–23). She was not present when God gave the gift to the man, so the man had to preach the word to the woman, his bride. Here we see a foreshadowing of Christ, the Second Adam, who preaches to His Bride, the church, so that she might receive the gifts of God: worship.

So when the risen Christ appeared to His disciples on the mountain at the place He had said He would be present with them, the disciples worshiped Him. They had gone there to receive the gifts He was going to give them. They were not on that mountain because they had determined it would be a great place to give Jesus their love, support, and devotion. They were not there to do something for Him. They were there to receive what He wanted to give them, which is what this book is really all about: the gifts Christ gave His church.

Receiving Gifts in the Divine Service

Because of the confusion that has come to exist about the word *worship*, we will use the phrase *Divine Service*. Think of it this way: The triune God—Father, Son, and Holy Spirit—serves us with His gifts. This is completely backward to the American way of thinking about worship, but it is the way the Bible speaks about worship. God comes to us with His gift of Holy Baptism, where we confess that we are by nature sinful and unclean and in need of His mercy, forgiveness, and salvation. He absolves us of our sins, creating peace between us and Him. Thus we join the angelic choir on the night of His birth, singing, "Glory to God in the highest, and on earth peace among those with whom He is pleased!" (Luke 2:14). He comes to us in His Word, as we hear from all the Scriptures, including the Old Testament, the Epistles, and most especially, the Holy Gospel accounts of the life of Christ, our Savior. We hear that Word of God expounded on in the sermon so that, by it, the Holy Spirit might nurture our faith and increase our understanding of what our Savior has done for us by His death and resurrection. Then we cry out to the One who hears our prayers, as He has exhorted us to do, and promises to hear us. We receive the very body and blood of Christ sacrificed on the cross, delivered to us in bread and wine for our forgiveness. Finally, we leave with the blessing He commanded in Numbers 6:24–26.

Gifts given. Gifts received. This is how the Bible defines worship: God coming to us to give His gifts to us poor beggars, who simply receive His gifts with thanksgiving and praise.

Who Doubted?

The second action is less clear. What does it mean that some doubted? This may be what I call a "pious pretension." We want the disciples to be models of faith—strong role models for us to aspire to be like. We struggle with disciples who are weak, who have doubts, who fail. After all, they are the *apostles*, the hand-picked-by-Jesus men who walked with Him for three years. We envision them wearing spandex and capes, indicating their status as "Super Apostles," with the letters *S* and *A* on their chests. We assume that after they spoke with the risen Christ Jesus in His glorified state, they had no doubts or questions as to who He was and why He had come to earth. They have to be super-hero-level disciples. There is no way that any of them doubted what was happening on that mountain. There must have been only a few, maybe just a couple of them, who had any doubts and risked losing their Super Apostle status. It just has to be this way.

Yet, when we read the four Gospel accounts closely, we quickly realize that the disciples were far from super, far from unshakable, and not-so-great role models. Peter is always example number one here. He jumped out of the boat on a stormy sea (only to begin to sink), boasted that he would never deny Jesus (only to do it three times), and swung a sword to separate Malchus from his ear. Thomas comes up quickly, too, with his unwillingness to believe Jesus was risen until he thrust his hand into his Lord's nail and spear wounds.

Judas betrayed Jesus in the Garden of Gethsemane. Then all the other disciples bolted. Only John was willing to stay with Jesus to the end. All of His other handpicked followers abandoned Jesus to His death.

In other words, they were just like you and me. We have all abandoned Jesus. That's one way to look at sin. When we sin, we abandon the good things God has sought to give us in His holy commands. Sin is replacing God with something we deem more important. It comes back to the First Commandment. We abandon the one true God for something we elevate into a god of our own making, giving it the fear, love, and trust we should be giving to God and God alone. And this is the reason Jesus came for the Twelve, for you, for me, for everyone. Jesus came to forgive all our sins, all the times we have abandoned God and replaced Him with something, anything, everything else.

Not only have we abandoned Jesus, but we have had doubts about what is written in the Scriptures regarding one thing or another. We all have had doubts about how God can exist in all eternity with no beginning and no end. That's because every other thing we experience in this world has a beginning and an end. Our limited human reason and understanding wrestle with God having no beginning and no end. We also have doubts about the globe-covering flood that killed all but eight people and one pair of every living thing. The parting of the Red Sea, the sun standing still, a donkey talking, or a man surviving for three days inside the belly of a fish also can cause us to question God's Word. Perhaps the hardest thing to believe is that

Jesus was willing to give up His place in heaven to come down to this little rock in the universe, endure the travails of living in this sinful world, and then suffer and die to save someone like you and me.

Doubt is part of being a sinner and saint at the same time. But doubts do not equal unbelief. Consider the father of the demon-possessed boy in Mark 9. After approaching the disciples, who could not help him, the father went to Jesus. The father cried, "I believe; help my unbelief!" (Mark 9:24). You can believe and still doubt. In all likelihood, you have experienced this very thing in your own life.

Some of the Eleven on that mountain did too. When you or I have doubts, we might imagine these apostles thumbing their noses at us and wagging their fingers, "How dare you have doubts? Be like us, never doubting, always believing, like perfect little angels." But this image is not true at all. When we have doubts, we are in good company—the company of the apostles and prophets and all those who have gone before us in faith.

What Did They Doubt?

It's not immediately clear what exactly they doubted. Let's look at verse 17 again:

> 17 And having seen Him,
> they worshiped,
> but some doubted.

(Voth)

When Jesus appeared to the Eleven on the mountain, they did two things: they worshiped, and some doubted.

Although the original text does not provide a direct object, we have no problem understanding that the object of the disciples' worship was Jesus. As we discussed, this was the appropriate thing to do in the presence of the Son of God. It's when we get to the second action that we struggle to understand the direct object, that is, what some of the Eleven were doubting. Again, pious pretension takes hold here: Our mind tells us that there is no way any of these eleven men would doubt Jesus, yet Matthew tells us that they did.

The "what" of doubting Him is less clear, but this is not rank unbelief, as if they stubbornly refused to believe in Jesus. Matthew 16 reveals in Peter's confession that they believed Jesus is the Son of God, the Messiah, even if they did not understand exactly what that meant.

Rev. Dr. Jeffery A. Gibbs states, "For my part, it seems likely that what caused their doubt was what lay ahead of them."[10] The disciples were certainly very concerned about what was ahead. In Acts 1:6, the disciples asked Jesus, "Lord, will You at this time restore the kingdom to Israel?" These close friends and many of His other followers were looking with Jewish eyes for a restoration of an earthly kingdom like David's. Perhaps they had doubts about Jesus' ability to restore it and what it meant for their future as leaders in that earthly kingdom.

10 Jeffrey A. Gibbs, *Matthew 21:1–28:20,* Concordia Commentary (Concordia Publishing House, 2018), 1630.

Rev. Dr. David Scaer states, "The reference to doubting should not be understood as the disciples having questions about the nature or actuality of His resurrection. This doubting involved confusion in the sense of 1) not fully understanding the significance of the resurrection for them and 2) the reason why Jesus had commanded them to come to Galilee."[11] Reading Matthew's Gospel with an eye on Luke's words in Acts gives way to this answer. Perhaps the disciples were wondering why Jesus had to die if He was planning to establish a political, earthly kingdom. Maybe they were pondering why they were in Galilee if Jerusalem was the place to reestablish the throne and kingdom of David. The location didn't make much sense. These two honorable professors have similar thoughts on what exactly the disciples were doubting.

Let's return to our context question. We are at the only post-resurrection appearance Jesus made to the disciples recorded in Matthew's Gospel. According to Matthew 28:1, only "Mary Magdalene and the other Mary went to see the tomb." The other Gospel narratives give us more details about the disciples' reaction to the news of Christ's resurrection and His first postresurrection visit. Mark says,

> Afterward He appeared to the eleven themselves as they were reclining at table, and He rebuked them for their unbelief and hardness of heart, because they had not believed those who saw Him after He had risen. (Mark 16:14)

11 David P. Scaer, "The Relation of Matthew 28:16–20 to the Rest of the Gospel," *Concordia Theological Quarterly* 55 (1991): 248.

Luke has significantly more to say about this subject:

> Now it was Mary Magdalene and Joanna and Mary the mother of James and the other women with them who told these things to the apostles, but these words seemed to them an idle tale, and they did not believe them. But Peter rose and ran to the tomb; stooping and looking in, he saw the linen cloths by themselves; and he went home marveling at what had happened. (Luke 24:10–12)

> As they were talking about these things, Jesus Himself stood among them, and said to them, "Peace to you!" But they were startled and frightened and thought they saw a spirit. And He said to them, "Why are you troubled, and why do doubts arise in your hearts? See My hands and My feet, that it is I Myself. Touch Me, and see. For a spirit does not have flesh and bones as you see that I have." And when He had said this, He showed them His hands and His feet. And while they still disbelieved for joy and were marveling, He said to them, "Have you anything here to eat?" They gave Him a piece of broiled fish, and He took it and ate before them. (Luke 24:36–43)

And finally, the testimony of John:

> So Peter went out with the other disciple, and they were going toward the tomb. Both of them were

> running together, but the other disciple outran Peter and reached the tomb first. And stooping to look in, he saw the linen cloths lying there, but he did not go in. Then Simon Peter came, following him, and went into the tomb. He saw the linen cloths lying there, and the face cloth, which had been on Jesus' head, not lying with the linen cloths but folded up in a place by itself. Then the other disciple, who had reached the tomb first, also went in, and he saw and believed; for as yet they did not understand the Scripture, that He must rise from the dead. (John 20:3–9)

Mark, Luke, and John all tell us that the disciples had doubts about Jesus' resurrection. They thought He was a ghost. They were shocked that Jesus, who had died by crucifixion, was now alive and well. This doesn't happen. Dead people don't come back from the dead. That's the second rule of being dead. You don't recover. Dead is dead.

But wait a second, you say. Elijah had raised the widow's son in 1 Kings 17. Jesus Himself raised Jairus's daughter (see Mark 5:21–43), the widow's son in Nain (see Luke 7:11–17), and, most notably, Lazarus (see John 11:38–44). These eleven men had seen Jesus bring dead people back to life not once, not twice, but three times. But there is one big difference between these instances of resurrection and Jesus' resurrection. In the aforementioned accounts, the disciples had watched Jesus bring people back from death to life. But in this case, Jesus was dead.

No one had the ability to raise Him. And dead people can't raise themselves back to life. That's the first rule of being dead.

Now, there are plenty of places in the New Testament where the writers refer to God the Father raising Jesus from the dead, including Acts 2:24; 4:10; 5:30; 10:40; Romans 10:9; Galatians 1:1; Colossians 2:12; and 1 Peter 1:21. In Romans 8:11, Paul says it was the Holy Spirit who raised Jesus from the dead. Notice that all of these were written after the events of the resurrection and the day of Pentecost. The disciples did not yet comprehend the nature of the Trinity's connection in raising Jesus from the dead. But what they should have had in mind was Christ's own words about His resurrection. Consider these words from Jesus:

> I am the good shepherd. The good shepherd lays down His life for the sheep. He who is a hired hand and not a shepherd, who does not own the sheep, sees the wolf coming and leaves the sheep and flees, and the wolf snatches them and scatters them. He flees because he is a hired hand and cares nothing for the sheep. I am the good shepherd. I know My own and My own know Me, just as the Father knows Me and I know the Father; and I lay down My life for the sheep. And I have other sheep that are not of this fold. I must bring them also, and they will listen to My voice. So there will be one flock, one shepherd. For this reason the Father loves Me, because I lay down My life that I may take it up again. No one takes it from Me, but I lay

> it down of My own accord. I have authority to lay it down, and *I have authority to take it up again.* This charge I have received from My Father. (John 10:11–18, emphasis added)

Jesus said that He was the one who would raise Himself from the dead. No one else in all of history can make this claim. Only Jesus had the power to lay down His own life in death for the sins of the world and bring Himself back from the dead. It is no wonder that the disciples had doubts that Jesus was risen from the dead when first encountering Him after the resurrection. Remember, doubt is not unbelief. They were simply confronted with something that does not happen unless you are dealing with Jesus, so it is very natural to say they had doubt as to how it could be that Jesus was risen from the dead. I believe all Eleven had doubts about how Jesus was alive again and was physically meeting with them on the mountain.

Law and Gospel

This dichotomy of worship and doubt teaches us two more important understandings of the Scriptures. The first is that God's Word comes to us in two ways. It comes to us as Law, that is, the commands of God. God's Law holds up a mirror to our lives to reflect how we have failed to live according to His good and perfect commands in our thoughts, words, and actions by the things we should not have done and the things we should have done. Paul states this function of the Law to Christians in Rome and to us:

> So the law is holy, and the commandment is holy and righteous and good.
>
> . . . For I do not understand my own actions. For I do not do what I want, but I do the very thing I hate. Now if I do what I do not want, I agree with the law, that it is good. So now it is no longer I who do it, but sin that dwells within me. For I know that nothing good dwells in me, that is, in my flesh. For I have the desire to do what is right, but not the ability to carry it out. For I do not do the good I want, but the evil I do not want is what I keep on doing. (Romans 7:12, 15–19)

This word of Law shows us that our sins are contrary to the Word of God.

The Word of God also comes to us in the message of the Gospel: We are saved by grace through faith in Christ Jesus, who bore our sins, doubts, and failures to keep the Law when He suffered and died on the cross for us. Christ Himself assures us, "Thus it is written, that the Christ should suffer and on the third day rise from the dead, and that repentance for the forgiveness of sins should be proclaimed in His name to all nations" (Luke 24:46–47).

Sinner and Saint

Worship and doubt, Gospel and Law direct us to the second important understanding of the Scriptures, which is hinted at in the passage from Romans 7. Paul talks about the struggle he faced daily, hourly, moment by moment:

- knowing what is good and right according to God's Law;
- knowing how to walk according to the Holy Spirit living and moving in him even as he battled with his old, sinful nature, which sought to rebel against God's Word.

In the Reformation tradition, this is captured beautifully by the Latin phrase *simul justus et peccator*, which means "simultaneously justified (saint) and sinner." Just as the Eleven worshiped and doubted at the same time, we, too, live our lives as those who are made righteous—justified by Christ—and who are simultaneously sinners. This dichotomy is difficult for us to comprehend. We are the new man, born from above in the waters of Holy Baptism with the Word and the indwelling of the Holy Spirit. Because we are justified by Christ, we delight in the Law of God and seek to live according to it. At the same time, we are the old Adam in that we have inherited sin from Adam and live in open rebellion against the Law of God by not living according to it.

This is one of the great geniuses of Martin Luther's teaching of the Ten Commandments in the Small Catechism. With two exceptions, Luther's explanations of the Commandments begin with what God forbids for our own good, defining how we sin against God's good commands. Then he addresses how we should live according to that same command since we are made new by the Holy Spirit. This pattern is summarized in this formula: "We should fear and love God so that we do not . . . but . . ." The two exceptions are the First and Sixth Commandments.

The First Commandment sets the stage for all the other commandments, as James says, "For whoever keeps the whole law but fails in one point has become guilty of all of it" (James 2:10). Thus Luther needs only to define how the saints of God keep this command. We are very good at creating gods of anything and everything else, so Luther did not need to elaborate on the prohibitions of the First Commandment. The Sixth Commandment is the same, and Luther's explanation contains instruction for how we are to live according to the new nature.

Dichotomies in Action

After meeting Jesus on the mountain in Galilee, the eleven disciples had two responses: doubt and worship. Gospel and Law. Saint and sinner. Each of these pairs are dichotomies—ideas or actions that are opposed to each other. Both are actions and resulting implications that are common to all of humanity in the presence of the Almighty. Rarely do these considerations enter into discussions of the Great Commission. I have never heard about the disciples' worship and doubt as part of the discussion of why Christians must go and make disciples. When the Great Commission is being discussed as the basis for mission work, this verse does not fit well with the rest of the emphasis. The way the Great Commission is taught in American Christianity requires you to cast all doubt aside, get rid of all fear and trepidation about talking to strangers (or, worse, family) about faith. You must be bold, you must be courageous, you must be like the Super Apostles on the mountain, ready to leap over huge obstacles to share Jesus with others. Nothing less will do.

Yet doubt is part of a Christian's life, and that is okay. Peter had doubts. Thomas had doubts. The whole band of disciples had doubts, yet they remained faithful disciples who listened to Jesus and believed in His words, even when they did not understand those words.

Just as the disciples were instructed by Jesus to meet Him at a designated place to hear Him, we, too, gather at the place Jesus has designated for hearing His Word. Jesus comes to us and is present with us in the Divine Service, speaking to us through the Word, the liturgy, the preaching and teaching, and the Sacraments. Christians gather as the church to hear Jesus and worship Him in reverent fear and awe. We come with our doubts. We have looked in the mirror of God's Law and have seen how we live our lives, and it is not pretty. That mirror of the Law may lead us to question how Jesus could love someone whose life is so ugly and messed up. The devil, the world, even our own sinful flesh tempt us to doubt that Jesus could forgive all our sins, especially the sin we fall into time and time again.

Yet Jesus has forgiven us, and He has gifts just waiting for us. That is the point of this farewell discourse, so keep reading!

DISCUSSION QUESTIONS

1. What is the difference between the modern American understanding of worship and what the Bible teaches about the Divine Service?

2. What did God give the children of Israel when they arrived at Mount Sinai?

3. What are some of the gifts the triune God gives us during the Divine Service?

4. How are the disciples described in the Gospel accounts, especially after Jesus' resurrection?

5. How does knowing that the disciples had doubts help you as a Christian?

6. What is the significance of the father's statement, "I believe; help my unbelief!" (Mark 9:24)?

7. How do the dichotomies of doubt and worship, Law and Gospel, sinner and saint help you rightly understand your life as a Christian?

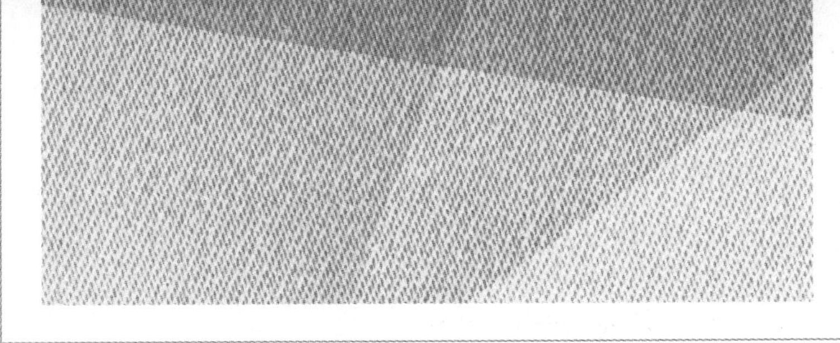

CHAPTER 4

Matthew 28:18

And Jesus came and said to them,
"All authority in heaven and on
earth has been given to Me."

After He arrived at the mountain with His disciples, who knew who He was and had worshiped Him, Jesus began His farewell discourse. It is telling that this verse is left out of many modern discussions of Jesus' Great Commission. Our Lord began not with a command or law that these men must fulfill or accomplish but with words of comfort. The risen Jesus had been given all authority in heaven and on earth. He was stating what He had accomplished by His death and resurrection in order to comfort His disciples, some of whom were having doubts and could really use comforting from their Lord.

Let's slow down and look more closely at this familiar text:

16The eleven disciples journeyed into Galilee
to the mountain which Jesus
designated to them,

[17]and having seen Him,
they worshiped,
but some doubted,
[18]and having drawn near,
Jesus spoke to them, saying,
"To Me has been given all authority
in heaven and
upon the earth."

(Voth)

God Comes to Us

Verse 18 starts with an important phrase: Jesus drew *near* to the Eleven. The text might imply that the disciples were hesitant to approach Jesus, perhaps because, as Luke says, they thought He was a spirit, a ghost (see Luke 24:36–43). So Jesus came to them. Think about worship again. We don't come to Jesus. He comes to us to give us His gifts, including His very presence in the Word and Sacraments.

The account in Matthew captures the first time they had seen Him after His death. It hearkens back to Luke's account of the Upper Room on that first Easter evening:

> As they were talking about these things, Jesus Himself stood among them, and said to them, "Peace to you!" But they were startled and frightened and thought they saw a spirit. And He said to them, "Why are you troubled, and why do doubts arise in your hearts? See My hands and My feet, that it is

> I Myself. Touch Me, and see. For a spirit does not have flesh and bones as you see that I have." And when He had said this, He showed them His hands and His feet. And while they still disbelieved for joy and were marveling, He said to them, "Have you anything here to eat?" They gave Him a piece of broiled fish, and He took it and ate before them. (Luke 24:36–43)

There is a recurring theme in the Gospel accounts about the first time Jesus appeared to His disciples after the resurrection. They were caught off guard by His presence, almost like they were paralyzed and unable to do or say anything. Jesus was the one who came to them and started the conversation. There was a beautiful juxtaposition in those encounters. The One who was dead and is now alive appears to those who are alive but appear dead.

The words of Christ always bring peace to troubled souls. Whether in the Upper Room or on the mountain in Galilee, in a boat in the middle of the stormy sea or at the empty tomb in a quiet garden, it was Jesus who came to His disciples with words of comfort that created peace and brought faith to those who were doubting His resurrection.

The reason Christ brings peace to troubled souls is because He has all authority. You could understand this as a blanket, general kind of authority over all things, and I don't think you'd be wrong. Jesus most certainly has all authority over all creation. Yet He added the words "in heaven and upon the earth," which sort of seems redundant, unless there is something else happening here that is omitted from many discussions of the Great Commission.

Authority to . . .

Let's go back to context. Matthew pointed to Jesus' authority earlier in his narrative. The first time we read about it is in chapter 7:

> And when Jesus finished these sayings, the crowds were astonished at His teaching, for He was teaching them as one who had authority, and not as their scribes. (Matthew 7:28–29)

Jesus had just finished His teaching on the mountainside that began with what is commonly called the Beatitudes. Several times Jesus said, "You have heard that it was said to those of old." Then He boldly added, "But I say to you . . ." (see Matthew 5:21). This signals that His teaching was unlike anything they had heard, with depth of meaning and heavenly power they had not experienced before. Even when He was just twelve years old, "all who heard Him were amazed at His understanding and His answers" (Luke 2:47). Understanding and wisdom were at the heart of what the people meant when they said Jesus' teaching had authority. We are not surprised by this because we know the conclusion: Jesus' teaching obviously had authority because He is God. He was the very Word of the Lord in the flesh (see John 1:1–3).

Like His words during the Sermon on the Mount, Jesus' final words on the mountainside had the power, wisdom, and authority of God, who created the heavens and the earth. Having the full authority of God gave power and credence to the instructions that followed. Yet the apostles who were doubting His resurrection needed comfort and assurance.

Jesus' authority is on full display in Matthew 8. A Roman centurion came to Jesus to plea for his paralyzed servant back home. Jesus offered to go to the man's home to heal the servant, but the centurion responded,

> Lord, I am not worthy to have You come under my roof, but only say the word, and my servant will be healed. For I too am a man under authority, with soldiers under me. And I say to one, "Go," and he goes, and to another, "Come," and he comes, and to my servant, "Do this," and he does it. (Matthew 8:8–9)

This Gentile recognized that Jesus had authority to heal his servant by simply speaking the word. What a testament to faith! Here again, you might hear the words of the apostle John:

> In the beginning was the Word, and the Word was with God, and the Word was God. He was in the beginning with God. All things were made through Him, and without Him was not any thing made that was made. (John 1:1–3)

This is Genesis 1 language, where God speaks the Word and it ***is***. The centurion understood that the God who created the universe with just a word was standing in front of him; all Jesus had to do in that situation was speak a word and it would be done. This sheds light on the farewell discourse, but it doesn't help us completely.

In chapter 1, we looked at Matthew 10, where Jesus gave the Twelve authority to cast out demons and heal the sick. This authority from Jesus is the same in both accounts in that it is from God the Son.

Matthew 9 and Mark 2 record the account of some men bringing their friend to Jesus. The man was paralyzed and laying on a bed. The house where Jesus was teaching was so full that the group could not enter through the door. Desperate and determined, they made a hole in the roof and lowered their friend down until he was in front of Jesus. When Jesus saw the man, He said, "Take heart, My son; your sins are forgiven" (Matthew 9:2). This caused an uproar with the scribes: "Who can forgive sins but God alone?" (Mark 2:7). The scribes were stating what they had learned from the Scriptures: Only God can forgive sins. The scribes also knew that God reigned from heaven. This was blasphemy, unless the Son of God had become incarnate and was standing before them, bodied and blooded in the form of man, and was walking, talking, teaching, healing, and saying that He was forgiving sins on earth. His answer confirmed His authority: "But that you may know that the Son of Man has authority on earth to forgive sins" (Matthew 9:6).

Because He is God, the Son of Man has the same authority as God in heaven to forgive sins on earth just as they are forgiven before the throne of God in heaven. This is because He, the Second Person of the Holy Trinity, is the one who will pay the price of sin with His death.

In Matthew 28, the Eleven, who had abandoned Jesus in Gethsemane, heard the message that He had the authority to forgive sins—*their* sins—on earth just as He did in heaven. This was of great comfort to them. They needed forgiveness from Jesus right then and there. This same comfort, this assurance that one's sins are forgiven on earth in the same way as they are forgiven in heaven, is foundational to how Christ would build His church and was the starting point for the proclamation of the church. Your sins are forgiven in Christ Jesus by His death on the cross!

Forgiveness in the Church

Even more amazing is that Jesus gave His authority to forgive sins to the church. Matthew 16 records that Jesus and His disciples were in Caesarea Philippi, which was far away from Jerusalem. Jesus asked His disciples two key questions:

- Who do the people say I am?
- Who do you say I am?

Peter, as spokesman for the whole group, confessed, "You are the Christ, the Son of the living God" (Matthew 16:16). At this confession, Jesus said to the Twelve,

> On this rock I will build My church, and the gates of hell shall not prevail against it. I will give you the keys of the kingdom of heaven, and whatever you bind on earth shall be bound in heaven, and whatever you loose on earth shall be loosed in heaven. (Matthew 16:18–19)

Notice the connection with the farewell discourse. Jesus had all authority to forgive sin in heaven and on the earth. Jesus had promised that He would give this authority to the church in chapter 16. In chapter 28, the gift was given as He instructed the Eleven how He would build His church. This parallels what we read in John's Gospel:

> And when He had said this, He breathed on them and said to them, "Receive the Holy Spirit. If you forgive the sins of any, they are forgiven them; if you withhold forgiveness from any, it is withheld." (John 20:22–23)

The passage from John records Jesus' first postresurrection visit to His disciples on the evening of His resurrection. Jesus highlighted the purpose for which He had been crucified, died, was buried, and was resurrected: the forgiveness of sins.

In Matthew 16, Jesus speaks of binding and loosing, or applying or removing chains. The locks shut, binding a person's hands and feet, and the key unlocks the chains, loosening them and setting the prisoner free. Forgiving sins is the same. By His death and resurrection, Christ Jesus loosens the chains of sin, death, and the power of the devil that ensnare and imprison each of us. This is His primary office, or role.

Christians are to forgive other people who are repentant. Matthew records an event between Jesus and Peter that clearly demonstrates the command to forgive so that the bonds of love may not be broken. Jesus taught His disciples, "If your brother sins against you, go and tell him his fault, between you and him alone. If he listens to you, you have gained your brother" (Matthew 18:15). Peter responded with a question for Jesus about his brother, possibly Andrew, who may have been present: "'Lord, how often will my brother sin against me, and I forgive him? As many as seven times?' Jesus said to him, 'I do not say to you seven times, but seventy-seven times'" (Matthew 18:21–22).

The church has the Christ-given power to forgive sins, but it also has the power to bind sins to sinners who do not repent and openly continue in unrepentant and disobedient ways. This authority was given to the church and her pastors by God.

The called, ordained pastor acts on behalf of the church to carry out the final words of Christ from Matthew 28, in accordance with Matthew 16 and John 20. God uses the vocal cords of the man in the office of pastor to announce His forgiveness—the loosing of sins on earth and before His throne in heaven.

The Comfort of Absolution

The authority to forgive sins in heaven and on the earth is the beginning of Jesus' farewell discourse. As noted, these words of comfort begin the discourse. The eleven disciples had gathered on the mountain in Galilee, and some were fighting against doubt. According to Matthew's account, the last time these men had been with Jesus was in the Garden of Gethsemane, where they had promised to never abandon Him. Yet they all failed to stay awake at His request while He prayed, and when the crowd came to arrest Jesus, they fled. Apart from John, they were nowhere to be found as He was unfairly accused and tried, as He endured public humiliation and indignity, as He was beaten and forced to carry His own cross to Golgoltha. They needed forgiveness.

Rather than commanding them to do something, Jesus began with forgiveness, comfort, assurance, and peace. Because of His sacrificial substitutionary death on the cross, the wages of sin, the price that sin extracts from all people, is now paid in full. By His resurrection, eternal life is restored. All who believe in Him will not face damnation and eternal death. This is Good News, the Gospel, and it must be shared. This is the basis for all that will follow. Without forgiveness of sins, there is no point in going any further. This is a great omission from most Great Commission discussions. Christ Jesus has the authority to forgive all sin. This forgiveness is what Jesus charged the disciples to communicate. Then Jesus told them how it would be done.

DISCUSSION QUESTIONS

1. Who initiated the conversation between Jesus and the disciples? What implication does this have in rightly understanding these verses and the Christian mission in general?

2. How does the account of the man who was paralyzed show Jesus' authority to forgive sins?

3. Why did Jesus begin His discourse with comfort, assurance, peace, and the Gospel? Why did the disciples need to hear that Jesus had the authority to forgive their sins?

4. How does Jesus' authority to forgive sins relate to the proclamation of the church?

5. What connections exist between Matthew 16 and Matthew 28?

6. Why is it important to communicate and deliver the forgiveness of sins to others?

7. What is the comfort you receive in Holy Absolution from Christ via your pastor?

CHAPTER 5

MATTHEW 28:19A

Go therefore and make
disciples of all nations.

Go. This little word is the whole emphasis of the modern interpretation of the Great Commission: I have to go! Jesus demands it! If I want to obey Him, I have to go on overseas mission trips. I have to tell people about Jesus at work or school. If I don't, they will never hear about Jesus.

Perhaps you have heard this language or similar words. This idealized version of the Great Commission prioritizes our doing, our efforts and achievements. Jesus never intended for these farewell verses to make people feel guilty, cause them to believe that if they don't tell others about Him, they will be responsible for all the people who end up in hell.

This contradicts the rest of the Scriptures. Remember what God said through His prophet Isaiah:

> For as the rain and the snow come down from heaven
> and do not return there but water the earth,

making it bring forth and sprout,
  giving seed to the sower and bread to the eater,
so shall My word be that goes out from My mouth;
  it shall not return to Me empty,
but it shall accomplish that which I purpose,
  and shall succeed in the thing for which I sent it.

(Isaiah 55:10–11)

God's Word does what God says it will do and accomplishes what He wants it to accomplish. Our part in this is simply to share the story of Jesus' salvation. God will create and sustain faith through that Word. This is not an excuse to never tell people about Jesus. Rather, this is a proper ordering of faith and understanding of what God does. It is God's work through His Word by His Holy Spirit that creates faith in people's hearts to believe in Jesus Christ for forgiveness and salvation. All the pressure is off of you and your doing. But you should rejoice that you have freedom in your life in accordance with your vocations to tell people about Jesus and invite them to the place where He is found. Go back to the account from Matthew 9:1–8 and Mark 2:1–12, when the men brought their friend to Jesus. This account defines our biblical role in Christian mission. You bring people to where Jesus is found, where He has said He will be found, at the place He designated—in His Word, Baptism, and Holy Communion. Let's develop that idea further.

Less than a Command

First let us fix what is perhaps one of the greatest translation tragedies in the text we are examining. The Greek word translated "Go" is not a one-time command, as if the disciples could complete the task by walking down the mountain and going back home. If you wanted to communicate the full meaning of the Greek, it would clumsily read, "having gone out and continuing to go out."

Here's how I would translate this in context:

16The eleven disciples journeyed into Galilee
to the mountain which Jesus
designated to them,
17and having seen Him,
they worshiped,
but some doubted,
18and having drawn near,
Jesus spoke to them, saying,
"To Me has been given all authority
in heaven and
upon the earth.
19Therefore, having gone out."

(Voth)

"Having gone out" implies a natural movement but not necessarily an intentional one. "Go" demands that you leave, that you pack your bags and walk away from where you are and journey to someplace new. That describes when the Holy Spirit set Paul and Barnabas aside and sent them on their missionary journeys. They had to be actively involved, planning their next step, making sure they were properly equipped to win people for Jesus. It is what missionaries do today.

"Having gone out" recognizes that you will move from your home to a different location. Work and education are two big reasons we might relocate. Persecution, both in the state and in the church, might cause people to leave their homes and move elsewhere. "Having gone out" is the natural flow of life that happens, often without recognizing that something has taken place. It's passive, merely going on, rather than a planned, intentional active heading out on a grand journey of a lifetime.

History tells us that Rome attacked Jerusalem within forty years of Jesus' farewell discourse, dispersing the Jewish people around the world. It's called the Diaspora. Many Christians who the Romans believed were part of a sect of Judaism were also scattered during this time. Thus "having gone out" from Jerusalem and Galilee into Gentile lands, they were scattered into other parts of the world to proclaim forgiveness in Jesus. That is how Christ fulfilled, and continues to fulfill, His promise to build His church, baptizing and making disciples.

As humanity continued to spread throughout and populate the globe, Christ's disciples established churches where God's Word would be taught and the Sacraments would be administered. This is only fitting. The first command God gave Adam and Eve was "Be fruitful and multiply and fill the earth" (Genesis 1:28). The same command was given to Noah after the flood. Even when man decided not to scatter, choosing instead to build a city with a tower reaching up to heaven, "the Lord dispersed them over the face of all the earth" (Genesis 11:9). We were meant to fill the earth, "having gone out" to establish places around the globe where people can gather to hear the Word of God and receive His gifts. That said, we don't have to go on a mission trip to Africa or South America or Asia to tell people about Jesus, although we certainly can. Our day-to-day ordinary lives are lived within a few miles of our homes in most cases. Within those miles, there is a church that faithfully preaches the Gospel in its truth and purity and administers the Sacraments according to Christ's command. Go to that place Christ has designated for us to hear Him and receive the forgiveness He has authorized the church to administer.

Motivations

A second element of the translation is the word *therefore*. This word always points out a cause-and-effect relationship. In other words, because of *A*, therefore *B*. *B* is the direct result of *A*. "Therefore" follows "all authority in heaven and on earth has been given to Me" (Matthew 28:18), making it the reason for "having gone out." Our going and making disciples is based on Christ's authority, on the Good News, the Gospel, of His forgiveness. In other words, because Christ has forgiven all your sins, you should want to go out to share this Good News with others so that they, too, may know His forgiveness.

But the Great Commission interpretation so common in modern Christianity takes the last two verses of Matthew 28

("Go therefore and make disciples . . .") out of context, separating it from verse 18. So, cut off from the authority given to Christ to forgive sins, "therefore" can only relate to "Go." Thus the modern interpretation turns "Go" into a command, and Christ's commission becomes Law instead of Gospel.

You may wonder why "therefore" is after "Go" in our translations. In the original Greek, the word *therefore* is a postpositive, "that is, it cannot stand first in its clause. Ordinarily it stands second."[12] In other words, in Greek sentence structure, *therefore* cannot be the first word of the sentence. (In English, we can let it stand first.) English translations stay as close to the Greek as possible, which permits "therefore" to follow "Go" yet refers to Christ receiving authority as cause. In English, you can say either "Therefore go and make disciples" or "Go therefore and make disciples." Both mean the same thing. The cause in Jesus' farewell discourse is not "Go." Rather, it is what we discussed in chapter 4, namely, that Jesus gives authority to the church to forgive sins.

This changes the reason or motivation for His farewell discourse. Jesus has all authority in heaven and on earth to forgive sinners; therefore, there is something to do. Because we have forgiveness, the church proclaims the forgiveness of sin by Jesus' authority in every place she has been scattered. The motivation is not "You must do this." The motivation is "Because Jesus has finished His work of salvation, now the church, having gone out in her daily vocations, shares this Good News." It is

12 J. Gresham Machen, *New Testament Greek for Beginners* (Macmillan, 1923), 44.

joyful activity not based on compulsion but on the freedom that comes from Christ. What an omission in the modern understanding of the Great Commission!

The First Command

The verb in the Greek in verse 19 is not "Go." Rather, the action of this sentence lies in the next part of the verse. The verb in the Greek is what we translate as "make disciples." It could also be simplified "to disciple," as in "instruct," which is how I translate the word. But there is more here. This verb is used to express the concept of causing someone to become a disciple. If *disciplize* was a real word, it would best match the tenor of the Greek. In other words, God sends forth His creative Word in grace through the gift of Jesus Christ to create faith, which in turn causes a person to become a believer. The process of making someone a disciple is God's work through His Word by the Holy Spirit. We will develop that more in chapter 6, lest we get ahead of ourselves in examining this event.

The question about who we should disciple has much to do with our context. Some review is needed here to help clarify what was happening in the farewell discourse. Before His death, Jesus sent His twelve disciples to the lost sheep of Israel to cast out demons, heal the sick, and proclaim the same message He was proclaiming in Matthew 10. Here in Matthew 28, after the resurrection, the Eleven were with Jesus on a mountain in Galilee in a Gentile region. The to whom implied in "having gone out" changes. Whereas Jesus sent them out among only the

Jews, the lost sheep of Israel, in Matthew 10, here He expanded their mission field in Matthew 28. Let's go back to the text:

> 19"Therefore, having gone out,
> disciple all the Gentiles."
>
> (Voth)

The disciples were surrounded by Gentiles and had previously only been sent to the lost sheep of the house of Israel; here, Jesus expanded the parameters regarding to whom the disciples were to preach. This is the bookend from the beginning of Matthew's Gospel account that is a great omission in most Great Commission discussions. As previously noted, Matthew included four outsiders in Jesus' genealogy—the four Gentile women: Tamar, Rahab, Ruth, and Bathsheba. By including these Gentiles in chapter 1 of his Gospel, Matthew foreshadowed what was happening in chapter 28. Just as in the past, when Gentiles were included in God's Old Testament church, so by the disciple-making work of these apostles and others, more Gentiles would be included in God's church of all time and place.

Of course this call to make disciples of Gentiles does not negate making disciples of the first group, namely the lost sheep, or children, of Israel. Instead of only reaching the Jews with Christ's Gospel, the disciples were to also reach the Gentiles. In other words, they were called to preach to both Jew and Gentile—"all nations" (Matthew 28:19). This is also a fine comparison to the parallel passage in Mark's Gospel:

> And He said to them, "Go into all the world and proclaim the gospel to the whole creation. Whoever believes and is baptized will be saved, but whoever does not believe will be condemned." (Mark 16:15–16)

Gentiles and the lost sheep of Israel, all nations, all creation—all ways to say the same thing. This message of salvation in Jesus is for all people, no matter their nationality, ethnic group, people group, or language. This is the foundation of John's revelation from Jesus Christ as he sees "a great multitude that no one could number, from every nation, from all tribes and peoples and languages, standing before the throne and before the Lamb" (Revelation 7:9). The Holy Christian Church, through the apostles having first gone out from this mountain in Galilee, would be scattered across the globe and include both Jews and Gentiles.

Jesus began His farewell discourse with the authority to forgive sins won by His death on the cross. He told the disciples that they would be scattered among the Gentiles from Ethiopia to India, according to church history—with the command to make disciples, or (better) cause people to become disciples of Christ Jesus.

How this will be done takes us into the next part of the text.

DISCUSSION QUESTIONS

1. What are the differences in emphasis between the standard understanding of these verses as the Great Commission versus as a farewell discourse?

2. What is the significance of using "having gone out" instead of "go"?

3. "Having gone out," where do you have the opportunity to make disciples?

4. How does the effect of the word *therefore* change when this verse is pulled out of its context? How does the word *therefore* change the motivation of the discourse when it is tied to Jesus' words in verse 18?

5. What is the difference in the motivations for proclaiming the Gospel from the Great Commission understanding and proclaiming it from the farewell discourse view?

6. What are the similarities and differences between Matthew 10 and Matthew 28?

7. If the Gospel is for Jews and Gentiles, who are we prohibited from sharing the Gospel with?

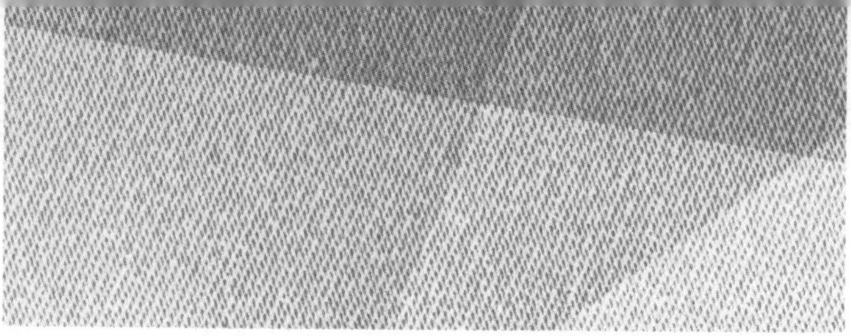

EXCURSUS

If Not "Go," Then What?

All right. I may have just shattered a popular motivation for mission work. I might even be accused of being antimissional. I am not. What I am concerned with is the abuse of one passage that is taken out of context to guilt-trip people into mission trips and street evangelism that benefits only the psyche of the person attempting to do something great for Jesus. Very few people enjoy it when a Jehovah's Witness or a missionary from the Church of Jesus Christ of Latter-day Saints comes knocking on the door selling their religion. Yet many times, well-meaning Christians, intentionally or unintentionally, have done the same thing. Jesus is not some commodity that requires door-to-door salesmanship. This misunderstanding of the Great Commission has caused heartache among people who have forced themselves out of their comfort zones because they think they must do this so they don't let Jesus down or jeopardize their eternal salvation. There must be a better way to approach the mission of Christ's church that doesn't place such a burden on people. Here is my suggestion.

Christ's Abiding Presence

In John 1, John the Baptizer was with two of his disciples near the Jordan River. As Jesus walked by, John pointed Him out to the two disciples and essentially said, "Look, there is the Lamb of God! Stop hanging out with me. Go with Him." They learned from John that salvation is found in Jesus. When Jesus asked what they wanted, they said, "'Rabbi' (which means Teacher), 'where are You staying?'" (v. 38). Jesus responded, "Come and you will see" (v. 39).

The original Greek has nuances that we miss in English, and John uses these nuances all the time. "Where are you staying?" is certainly what the disciples asked Jesus that day. The word translated as "stay" can also be translated "abide" or "remain," depending on the context. It would sound strange to our modern English ears to hear the disciples ask, "Jesus, where are You abiding?" Yet, when we look at the larger context of John's Gospel, the word *abide* appears time and time again:

- [Jesus said:] Whoever feeds on My flesh and drinks My blood has eternal life, and I will raise him up on the last day. For My flesh is true food, and My blood is true drink. Whoever feeds on My flesh and drinks My blood *abides* in Me, and I in him. As the living Father sent Me, and I live because of the Father, so whoever feeds on Me, he also will live because of Me. (John 6:54–57, emphasis added)

- So Jesus said to the Jews who had believed Him, "If you *abide* in My word, you are truly My disciples, and you will know the truth, and the truth will set you free." (John 8:31–32, emphasis added)

- [Jesus said:] *Abide* in Me, and I in you. As the branch cannot bear fruit by itself, unless it *abides* in the vine, neither can you, unless you *abide* in Me. I am the vine; you are the branches. Whoever *abides* in Me and I in him, he it is that bears much fruit, for apart from Me you can do nothing. If anyone does not *abide* in Me he is thrown away like a branch and withers; and the branches are gathered, thrown into the fire, and burned. If you *abide* in Me, and My words abide in you, ask whatever you wish, and it will be done for you. By this My Father is glorified, that you bear much fruit and so prove to be My disciples. As the Father has loved Me, so have I loved you. *Abide* in My love. If you keep My commandments, you will *abide* in My love, just as I have kept My Father's commandments and *abide* in His love. These things I have spoken to you, that My joy may be in you, and that your joy may be full. (John 15:4–11, emphasis added)

As you can see here, "Where are You abiding?" would bring more to light than just "Where are You staying?" Christ abides or stays or dwells in a location, and we are called to abide or stay or dwell in that place as well. When Andrew and the other disciple asked, "Where are You staying?" they were wondering where He was eating and sleeping. In other words, they were wondering where He was staying each night. Yet when we read theologically, the question is much deeper than simply where He was sleeping that night.

We need to know where Jesus is abiding. John recorded for us the exact place where Jesus is abiding—the Sacrament of Holy Communion, according to Jesus' words in John 6 and 8. We find the Word and Sacraments abiding in the Divine Service. We can read and study Christ's Word in our homes, at the lake, on a plane, and a host of other places, especially with a Bible app. But we can only hear the Word preached into our ears—according to Christ's command—and receive Christ's crucified body and blood, which then abides in us through actual physical eating and drinking in the Sacrament, in the Divine Service.

Come and See

When Jesus was asked where He was abiding, He extended the invitation, "Come and you will see" (John 1:39). Once he knew where Jesus was abiding, Andrew went to find Peter. Andrew told Peter, "We know where the Christ is abiding." Then he brought him to Jesus (see vv. 41–42).

The next day Jesus set off for Galilee. In John 1, it's very clear that Jesus was heading to Galilee. It's not as clear in the Greek who found Philip. It could have been Jesus or Andrew. Back up a couple of verses. John writes, "He *first* found his own brother Simon and said to him, 'We have found the Messiah' (which means Christ)" (v. 41, emphasis added). You may be tempted to read this as the very first action Andrew took, as in the first time Andrew went and found someone else, and then there was a second time that he did the same thing. It could be, and the Greek text would allow this, that before Jesus decided to go north to Galilee, Andrew went a second time to share the good news of finding the Messiah. Andrew, "having gone out," found Philip and brought Philip to Jesus, who then said to him, "Follow Me."

Philip, in response to being brought by Andrew to see where the Messiah was abiding, went out to find Nathanael and told him, "We know where the Christ is abiding" (see v. 45). When Nathanael resisted this new information (see v. 46), Philip invited Nathanael with words we have heard before: "Come and see." In his Concordia Commentary on John, Rev. Dr. William C. Weinrich sees a Semitic (Hebrew) force behind Philip's response that could be better if translated "*if* you come, *then* you will see."[13] When people have questions about who Jesus is and what He has done, the best place to find out the truth is not the internet. They need to be invited to come and see, to come and hear from the Holy Scriptures, from trained pastors and teachers, that Jesus is who He says He is and accomplished what He said He would—their salvation by His death. If they come, then they will see. This is the invitation to Nathanael and all who have questions about Jesus' credibility.

When Nathanael went to the place where Jesus was abiding, the Lord spoke, and faith was created in Nathanael, who confessed, "Rabbi, You are the Son of God! You are the King of Israel!" (v. 49). Having come to the place Jesus was abiding, by

13 William C. Weinrich, *John 1:1–7:1*, Concordia Commentary (Concordia Publishing House, 2015), 269. Emphasis in original.

the word of the incarnate Word, faith was created in Nathanael, as the promise of God declares,

> For as the rain and the snow come down from heaven
> and do not return there but water the earth,
> making it bring forth and sprout,
> giving seed to the sower and bread to the eater,
> so shall My word be that goes out from My mouth;
> it shall not return to Me empty,
> but it shall accomplish that which I purpose,
> and shall succeed in the thing for which I sent it.
>
> (Isaiah 55:10–11)

There is a pattern of missions forming here in the first chapter of John's Gospel. Let's keep going.

Bring Them to Jesus

John 4 records that Jesus encountered a woman of Samaria at Jacob's well. Jesus and His disciples had been traveling for some time. They arrived at the well, and Jesus, being tired in His humanity, sat down to abide by the well. While He was abiding there, a woman from the village came to get water. We often see this passage as the proof text for the "meeting people where they are" approach to missions. We have to go to the places people are rather than expect them to come to church. Notice carefully the sequence of events. Jesus sat down, and the woman came to where Jesus was. He did not go looking for her. She was not looking for Him. She arrived at the place where He was abiding at that moment.

A long dialogue ensued in which the woman's sin was exposed and faith was created. Emboldened by this new faith abiding in her, the woman returned to the village and said to the people, "Come, see" (v. 29). There was some doubt in her faith, but as we have discussed, doubt is not necessarily unbelief. She knew she had found the Messiah, the Christ of promise, and she couldn't wait to share this with others, to invite them to the place the Christ abided in so that they would also believe: "For we have heard for ourselves, and we know that this is indeed the Savior of the world" (v. 42).

In Matthew's Gospel, we looked at the account of the man who was paralyzed. Jesus forgave his sins, which caused an uproar among the religious leaders. We concluded that the authority Jesus has in heaven and on earth is to forgive sins. We can also consider this account in Mark from a biblical approach to missions. The account begins,

> And when He returned to Capernaum after some days, it was reported that He was at home. And many were gathered together, so that there was no more room, not even at the door. And He was preaching the word to them. And they came, bringing to Him a paralytic carried by four men. (Mark 2:1–3)

Jesus, the Word made flesh, was preaching the Word to them. How amazing that must have been! He was abiding in a house, mostly likely the home of Simon Peter (see Mark 1:29).

Four men brought their friend to the place where Jesus abided because their friend was not able to come to Jesus on his own. His legs were as good as dead. According to our sinful human nature, we are like this paralyzed man, dead and unable to go looking for Jesus or get ourselves to the place where Jesus is abiding.

We cannot come to Jesus on our own. Nor do we want to. The sinful mind is hostile toward God. It is an enemy that will not seek Him out or come to Him; instead, loving the darkness of sin, it will remain in the dark and avoid the light of Christ. Your family, friends, neighbors, coworkers, and classmates who do not know Jesus as Lord and Savior are not going to look for Him. They likely won't come to your church just because you say, "Hey, you should come to my church." They need to be brought to the place where Christ Jesus is abiding. Your invitation to come and see should include you bringing them in your vehicle to the place where you know Jesus is abiding. This gives you a chance to explain the Divine Service to them before they participate in the liturgy, and it allows them to ask questions on the way back home.

This pattern of people bringing others to Jesus is repeated over and over in the Gospels. Time and time again we read about people bringing people who were sick, people who couldn't walk, people who couldn't speak, and people who were possessed by demons to Jesus, hoping that He would heal them. The common Greek word for "heal" is the same word for "save." In the context of a restoration of health, we understand that to be a physical healing, but there is also a theological aspect. Christ Jesus is the one who heals us spiritually, the one who saves us from sin, death, and everlasting condemnation. When we bring our family, friends, neighbors, and others to the place where Jesus abides in His Word and Sacrament, through the preaching of His Word and distribution of His Meal, Christ heals them of their greatest infirmity: the sickness of sin that leads to death and eternal separation from God.

"Having gone out" from the place where Christ abides to our family, friends, coworkers, classmates, and neighbors, we invite them to come and see, knowing that if they come, then they will see by faith.

Missions is best understood as inviting and bringing others to the place where Christ is found so that they might hear His Word, be baptized, and be catechized in all His teachings. Now we turn to this process of making disciples.

DISCUSSION QUESTIONS

1. How is "abide" used throughout John's Gospel?

2. Where do you find Jesus abiding today?

3. What does Christ's abiding presence mean in your life?

4. Compare and contrast "Go and make" and "Come and see." Which one is more freeing and joyous for you as a Christian?

5. How does the sequence of events at Jacob's well challenge the idea of meeting people where they are in missions?

6. How did doubt play a role in the woman at the well's faith?

7. The man who was paralyzed was brought by his friends to where Jesus was abiding. How does this relate to missions today?

CHAPTER 6

MATTHEW 28:19B

Baptizing them in the name
of the Father and of the Son
and of the Holy Spirit.

The second half of this verse and the next verse address how the church communicates the message of Jesus Christ and Him crucified to other people. Jesus doesn't just magically make people believe in Him. Nor do people cause themselves to believe in Him. God uses means, instruments, earthly things to convey His forgiveness and message to earthly people. The Holy Spirit is the ultimate cause of a person becoming a disciple. Yet God has chosen us, His church, as the instrument through which He works as we teach, instruct, and catechize people in "the faith that was once for all delivered to the saints" (Jude 3).

Baptize Them, the First Command

The first part of causing people to become disciples is to baptize them in the name of the triune God. Matthew 28:19 is the key verse to understanding Christian Baptism.

"To baptize" comes from a Greek word that simply means "to apply water," often in a religious or ceremonial way. How much water is never specified. John the Baptizer was baptizing people at the edge of the wilderness along the Jordan River—a place in an arid land that had accessible water all the time. It makes sense that the person being baptized would be immersed in the river. However, scholars believe that the location where John was baptizing people in the Jordan River was not very deep. Full immersion may have been difficult, so he may have had each person bend over or kneel as he scooped handfuls of water and poured it over their head.

The application of water occurs elsewhere in the New Testament:

> For the Pharisees and all the Jews do not eat unless they wash [baptize] their hands properly, holding to the tradition of the elders, and when they come from the marketplace, they do not eat unless they wash [baptize]. And there are many other traditions that they observe, such as the washing [baptizing] of cups and pots and copper vessels and dining couches. (Mark 7:3–4)

Whether referring to the washing of hands before meals or the washing of cups, pots, copper vessels, and dining couches, the Greek word is *baptizo*, the root of the English word *baptize*. Think about that for a moment. In an arid land where water had to be drawn from wells, it makes no logical sense to fully immerse a "dining couch." To baptize, that is, to ceremonially wash to make religiously clean the items Mark references, the proper understanding would be that they sprinkled water onto these items in accordance with the tradition of the elders.[14] This baptizing didn't involve much water—a palmful at most. Therefore, the amount of water used for Christian Baptism is not central to Jesus' instructions. To baptize—to apply water with His Word—is at the heart.

In Christian Baptism, the command is to use water in any amount along with Christ's own words: "In the name of the Father and of the Son and of the Holy Spirit." This is Christ giving, or instituting, the gift of Holy Baptism to His church.

There are many verses in the New Testament we could cite regarding what Baptism is and its benefits for those who are baptized. Among them are the following:

- Whoever believes and is baptized will be saved, but whoever does not believe will be condemned. (Mark 16:16)
- Do you not know that all of us who have been baptized into Christ Jesus were baptized into His death? We were buried therefore with Him by baptism into death, in order that, just as Christ was raised from the dead by the glory of the Father, we too might walk in newness of life. (Romans 6:3–4)
- He saved us, not because of works done by us in righteousness, but according to His own mercy, by the

14 The tradition of the elders were the commands the Jews said God gave Moses on Mount Sinai. These were not written down but passed on orally from generation to generation.

washing of regeneration and renewal of the Holy Spirit, whom He poured out on us richly through Jesus Christ our Savior. (Titus 3:5–6)

- When the patience of God waited in the days of Noah, *while* an ark was being constructed, in which a few—that is, eight souls—were rescued through water. And also, corresponding to *this*, baptism now saves you, not the removal of dirt from the flesh, but an appeal to God for a good conscience through the resurrection of Jesus Christ. (1 Peter 3:20–21 LEB)

These wonderful verses for our consideration and understanding of Holy Baptism inspired Martin Luther to write the following:

What benefit does Baptism give?

It works forgiveness of sins, rescues from death and the devil, and gives eternal salvation to all who believe this, as the words and promises of God declare.

Which are these words and promises of God?

Christ our Lord says in the last chapter of Mark: "Whoever believes and is baptized will be saved, but whoever does not believe will be condemned." (Mark 16:16)

How can water do such great things?

Certainly not just water, but the word of God in

> and with the water does these things, along with the faith which trusts this word of God in the water. For without God's word the water is plain water and no Baptism. But with the word of God it is a Baptism, that is, a life-giving water, rich in grace, and a washing of the new birth in the Holy Spirit, as St. Paul says in Titus, chapter three: "He saved us through the washing of rebirth and renewal by the Holy Spirit, whom He poured out on us generously through Jesus Christ our Savior, so that, having been justified by His grace, we might become heirs having the hope of eternal life. This is a trustworthy saying." (Titus 3:5–8)
>
> **What does such baptizing with water indicate?**
>
> It indicates that the Old Adam in us should by daily contrition and repentance be drowned and die with all sins and evil desires, and that a new man should daily emerge and arise to live before God in righteousness and purity forever. (Small Catechism, Baptism, Second, Third, and Fourth Parts)

The Scripture passages above are the reason Christ instructs His church to baptize as He causes people to become His disciples. We are not baptized Lutheran or Roman Catholic or Methodist or Orthodox Presbyterian. We are baptized Christian, which means "belonging to Christ." In the waters of Holy Baptism, by God's Word, we are marked as belonging to

Christ, sealed for the day of redemption (see Ephesians 1:13). It is Christ's work with the Father and the Holy Spirit, using the hands and voice of the pastor on behalf of the church.

Born Again, Born from Above

Here we dig deeper into Christ's teaching about Holy Baptism as recorded in John 3 to aid our understanding of His final discourse in Matthew 28.

The account in John 3 begins with Nicodemus asking Jesus who He is. Jesus responded to him, "Truly, truly I say to you, unless someone is born from above, he is not able to see the kingdom of God" (John 3:3 LEB). Nicodemus's response revealed that he had a misunderstanding about being born again.

When I teach about this encounter, I ask people how they hear the word *bass*. I think of the instrument I played in high school. Other people think of a fish. It's the same four letters, different pronunciation, completely different objects. Again, we always come back to context. Next I have people ask me, "Where are my keys?" This example works well in conversation but not on paper because I answer, "They're in my bag" or "There, in my bag." Using homophones (*they're* and *there*) helps make the point in John 3:3.

The conversation between Jesus and Nicodemus demonstrates the complexity of spoken language. The Greek word Jesus uses for "from above" is the same Greek word Nicodemus heard and understood as *again*. As I noted in chapter 5, John loved to use words to their fullest, and there often is a double meaning in his writing. Jesus was speaking about a spiritual birth from above, that is, from God, as John writes in 1:12–13. Nicodemus was thinking about an earthly birth, as in a second birth from his mother. To be "born from above" is the language of Holy Baptism, as Jesus clearly said: "Born of water and the Spirit" (John 3:5).

"That which is born of the flesh is flesh, and that which is born of the Spirit is spirit," Jesus said (v. 6). Here is the point of comparison. Flesh gives way to flesh; that is, it's earthly. Spirit gives way to Spirit; that is, it's heavenly. This earthly and heavenly theme runs for the rest of the encounter and is the foundation of the argument Jesus made.

When talking about birth, there is the earthly, flesh birth that comes as a result of your parents' sexual activity, or as John suggests in John 1, born as a result of the desire of the flesh or a husband's will (see John 1:13). You had nothing to do with your earthly conception and birth. You can never cause yourself to be born. It is just not possible. In the same way, your heavenly birth from above, the Spirit birth, came not as a result of your choosing or accepting to be born, but of God's will. Said another way, this birth from above, Holy Baptism, is not something you can do any more than you could conceive or be born of yourself. It is the work of God through His Word.

The conversation does not end there but keeps the earthly and heavenly theme going. Nicodemus was "a ruler of the Jews" (John 3:1). Jesus drew a parallel of earthly and heavenly again (see vv. 14–15) by pointing to an event from history. In

Numbers 21, we read the account of the children of Israel rebelling against God and Moses again:

> From Mount Hor they set out by the way to the Red Sea, to go around the land of Edom. And the people became impatient on the way. And the people spoke against God and against Moses, "Why have you brought us up out of Egypt to die in the wilderness? For there is no food and no water, and we loathe this worthless food." Then the LORD sent fiery serpents among the people, and they bit the people, so that many people of Israel died. And the people came to Moses and said, "We have sinned, for we have spoken against the LORD and against you. Pray to the LORD, that He take away the serpents from us." So Moses prayed for the people. And the LORD said to Moses, "Make a fiery serpent and set it on a pole, and everyone who is bitten, when he sees it, shall live." So Moses made a bronze serpent and set it on a pole. And if a serpent bit anyone, he would look at the bronze serpent and live. (Numbers 21:4–9)

God sent venomous snakes among the people to discipline them for their grumbling. The snakes bit people, regardless of their age, and many died. When the people confessed their sin, God told Moses to make a likeness of the snake and lift it up on a pole. Then, whenever a person was bitten, they would look in faith at the image lifted up and be saved, regardless of their age once again. This earthly example from history was one Nicodemus could understand.

Jesus told Nicodemus and us that the same thing would happen when He was lifted up. This is the heavenly comparison to the earthly history. Just as the Israelites carried the venom of the fiery serpents, we carry the venom of the ancient snake in the form of our sinful nature, which causes us to rebel and sin against God, resulting in our deserved death, regardless of age. David confessed,

> Against You, You only, have I sinned
> and done what is evil in Your sight,
> so that You may be justified in Your words
> and blameless in Your judgment.
> Behold, I was brought forth in iniquity,
> and in sin did my mother conceive me.
>
> (Psalm 51:4–5)

God, in His mercy, has once again provided salvation. His only-begotten Son, Jesus, was lifted up on the pole of the cross in order that "whoever believes in Him may have eternal life" (John 3:15). Just as the children of Israel received an earthly salvation by looking in faith at the snake that was lifted up, you and I receive a heavenly salvation by looking in faith at Jesus, who was lifted up on the cross.

In this account, we see the connection between Holy Baptism and His crucifixion. The gift of salvation that Jesus won on the cross is delivered to us in Holy Baptism. Jesus connects the two, which Paul echoes in his letter to the church in Rome:

> We were buried therefore with Him by baptism into death, in order that, just as Christ was raised from the dead by the glory of the Father, we too might walk in newness of life.
>
> For if we have been united with Him in a death like His, we shall certainly be united with Him in a resurrection like His. (Romans 6:4–5)

The sinful grumbling of the Israelites referenced in Numbers 21 points to the sinful nature we inherited in our earthly birth. The salvation God offered Israel through the bronze serpent in Numbers 21 points to the salvation He offers us through Christ being lifted up on the cross, dying, and rising again so we will receive the gifts of forgiveness and eternal life through Him. That salvation is ours through the gift of Holy Baptism—the spiritual heavenly birth.

This is why the first part of causing someone to become a disciple is to baptize them "in the name of the Father and of the Son and of the Holy Spirit." In the waters of Holy Baptism, God's Word begets us from above, connecting us to the death, burial, and resurrection of Jesus so "that whoever believes in Him should not perish but have eternal life" (John 3:16).

But we are not to baptize them and forget them, leave them as orphans with no one to feed them. Jesus knew this, so He commanded us to do a second thing in the causation of becoming a disciple.

DISCUSSION QUESTIONS

1. What is the basic meaning of the Greek word *baptizo*, which is transliterated in English as *baptize*?

2. What is the important part of Christian Baptism? The age it happens, the amount of water that is used, or fulfilling the command of Jesus? Why?

3. Why did Nicodemus misunderstand Jesus' statement about being "born from above"?

4. Like Nicodemus's misunderstanding of Jesus' statement, what other examples can you think of that involve a play on words and meanings?

5. What is the connection between earthly birth and heavenly birth?

6. What historical event did Jesus use to draw a parallel between earthly and heavenly salvation? What is the connection to Jesus being lifted up?

7. What is the connection between Holy Baptism and Jesus' crucifixion?

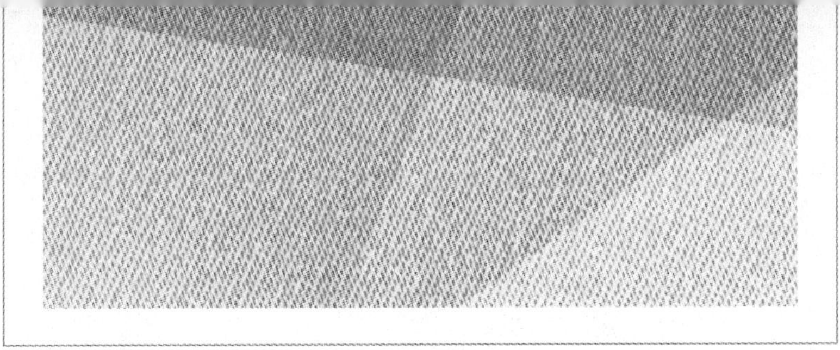

CHAPTER 7

Matthew 28:20a

Teaching them to observe
all that I have commanded you.

The first part of causing someone to become a disciple is covering them in the waters of Baptism with Christ's words. The second part is that they must be taught, instructed, or catechized. Baptism is a one-time event with an ongoing reality, just like our physical birth. Just as we are physically born only once, so we only have one spiritual birth through Baptism. Being born of the flesh is not the final step of life. We eat and drink, we grow and learn. Being born from above is not the final step either. In His farewell discourse, Jesus added the command that His beloved children were to be cared for throughout their earthly life, nurtured from cradle to grave as they grow and learn through instruction. The command to teach, to instruct people in the Word of God is echoed in the words of Peter's first epistle: "Like newborn infants, long for the pure spiritual milk, that by it you may grow up into salvation" (1 Peter 2:2). The analogy of Jesus' encounter with Nicodemus and His farewell discourse fit well with Peter's exhortation. We have a spiritual birth that requires feeding, just like our physical birth requires sustenance. We see the need for proper nutrition in both the earthly and heavenly.

Everyone will admit that a constant diet of donuts, lattes, soda, and candy bars is not good for you. If you put only bad foods into your body, bad things will happen to it. When your body is given proper nutrition, it grows in a healthy way. This analogy, like any analogy, has limits. You could eat the healthiest diet in the proper amounts and still get sick, die of cancer, or develop ALS. Yet Peter's exhortation is clearly understood. If you stick to solid, biblical preaching and teaching, your faith in Jesus Christ, who died on the cross and rose from the dead for your salvation, will be nourished and deepened. Listen to how Paul expresses this truth to Timothy:

> But as for you, continue in what you have learned and have firmly believed, knowing from whom you learned it and how from childhood you have been acquainted with the sacred writings, which are able to make you wise for salvation through faith in Christ Jesus. All Scripture is breathed out by God and profitable for teaching, for reproof, for correction, and for training in righteousness. (2 Timothy 3:14–16)

All Scripture, originating with the triune God, is useful for teaching, training, and feeding you from the time of infancy until you take your last earthly breath. God's Word is the source of your life as a Christian and sustains you. Like all food, it is best consumed daily by spending time reading God's Word, reading or hearing daily devotions from sources that are faithful to Scripture, listening to sermons, and so on.

There are a lot of resources that teach a perversion of God's Word. These are like candy and soda. They look appealing. They might even taste good at first, telling you all sorts of wonderful things. They will wave the Bible in one hand as the other hand pushes lies at you. If you spend any time on social media, you will see memes that sound like Bible passages but that take the passage out of—you guessed it—context. You may see memes that appear to be in line with biblical teachings but have nothing to do with the actual teachings of Jesus Christ. This is exactly what Paul warned Timothy about:

> For the time is coming when people will not endure sound teaching, but having itching ears they will accumulate for themselves teachers to suit their own passions, and will turn away from listening to the truth and wander off into myths. (2 Timothy 4:3–4)

This is why you need pure milk, good spiritual food that will result in furthering your understanding of salvation through Christ Jesus. Your diet should not come from a multitude of internet sources but from your doctor or dietitian. You need to feast on one source: Jesus. You need His Word, all of His Word, from "In the beginning . . ." to "The grace of the Lord Jesus be with all. Amen" (Genesis 1:1; Revelation 22:21).

Teach Them, the Second Command

This brings us back to Jesus' farewell discourse and His command to teach. Let's consider Christ's words from Matthew 28 again, as I have been translating them:

> 19"Therefore, having gone out,
> disciple all the Gentiles,
> baptizing them
> in the name of the Father and
> of the Son and
> of the Holy Spirit,
> 20teaching them
> to guard all things whatsoever
> I have decreed to you."
>
> (Voth)

Having gone out into the world, the church is to baptize in the name of the Father, Son, and Holy Spirit, and to teach people "to guard all things" that Jesus has given to His church. The traditional command "teaching them to obey" can be misconstrued into the "you must do this" mentality I am seeking to correct throughout this book. Jesus' command is to keep, guard, and make what He has said from beginning to end the most treasured possession you have.

The Holy Scriptures provide you with the best news that has ever been announced in all of history. Your sins are forgiven by

God Himself, on earth and in heaven, because of His Son's sacrifice on the cross. This is the Good News that the whole angel army left heaven to announce to the shepherds on the night of our Savior's birth. Just as Mary treasured in her heart all that happened around the birth of Jesus, we are called to treasure the Word of God, the Holy Scriptures, as the most incredible thing that has ever been given to us. And not just the parts we like—the whole thing. We should even treasure those difficult passages we find hard to understand, and especially those teachings the world and our human nature do not like.

We need to hold on to and treasure everything in our hearts Jesus said and taught, everything He commanded and decreed, the whole of the Scriptures in all the parts to guard and defend against all the attacks of Satan, the world, and even our sinful flesh. All of it. Remember: "*All* Scripture is breathed out by God and profitable for teaching, for reproof, for correction, and for training in righteousness" (2 Timothy 3:16, emphasis added).

If we are to guard all of Scripture and make it our most treasured possession, then we need to be rightly instructed and catechized in what Christ has said. We do not need to hear speculation, what-ifs, or maybes about things that God does not tell us directly in His Word. We need to hear about Jesus as the Holy Scriptures reveal Him to us. We don't need to hear about the latest trends in the culture and whitewash them with some biblical passages that sort of prove a point. We need Jesus, crucified and risen for the forgiveness of our sins. Jesus knows this is what we need, so He has made sure that the church's pastors know what they are supposed to preach and teach—"all things I have decreed to you."

Dr. Luther makes this point well:

> Again, in Mark, the last chapter [16:15], where Christ was sending out the disciples to preach, let us hear how he gives them commandment, sets a limit to their teaching, and bridles their tongues when he says, "Go into all the world and preach the gospel to every creature. He who believes will be saved," etc. He does not say, "Go and preach what you like, or what you think to be right." But he puts his own word into their mouth and bids them preach the gospel.
>
> He says the same thing again in the last chapter of Matthew [28:19], "Go and teach all nations, baptizing them in the name of the Father and of the Son and of the Holy Spirit, teaching them to observe all that I have commanded you." See, here again he does not say, "Teach them to observe what you invent," but what I have commanded you.[15]

Teach and preach what Jesus commanded, what He entrusted to us in the Word from beginning to end. Not my thoughts. Not your ideas. His. If your pastor or Bible study leader is saying something like, "I think what Jesus is saying here" or "What

15 Martin Luther, *Luther's Works*, vol. 35, *Word and Sacrament I*, ed. E. Theodore Bachmann and Helmut T. Lehmann (Fortress Press, 1960), 148.

I think this means," seek clarification that includes Scripture and respected Bible scholarship. Our Lord God gave us what He wanted us to know in His Word. We can trust this inerrant Word of God without adding our own ideas and imaginings.

The Threefold Enactment

The eleven disciples clearly understood this and proclaimed Christ's words to the church. Not long after the day of Pentecost, likely within just two months of Jesus' farewell discourse, Luke recorded what the church looked like and what it did. In Acts 2:42 (the same chapter that teaches us about Pentecost), we read,

> They were devoting themselves
> to the teachings of the apostles
> and to bread-breaking fellowship
> and to the Prayers.
>
> Reverence came to every soul.
> Many wonders
> and signs were done through the apostles.
> All the believers were together
> and held in common all things.
>
> (Voth)

On the day of Pentecost, three thousand people were added to the body of believers through Baptism. They gathered together with one purpose expressed by three activities.

First, they devoted themselves to the "teachings of the apostles," which is the doctrine Jesus Himself proclaimed to them. The apostles never thought to teach themselves or their own ideas; as Paul states, "We preach Christ crucified" (1 Corinthians 1:23). The teachings of the apostles is Luke's way of saying "teaching them to guard all things I have decreed to you." The parallels are clear: Jesus commanded the apostles to teach, and so they were teaching what He had given or decreed to them. The "you" of Matthew 28:20 clearly means the apostles, so Luke boiled down Jesus' words in the discourse to the simple phrase "the teachings of the apostles." "Teaching to guard all things I have decreed" can be simplified even further to one word: *doctrine*. As a matter of fact, the word in Greek for *doctrine* is used in its verb form and translated as "teaching" in Matthew 28:20 and Acts 2:42. Doctrine refers to the teachings of the Christ that are passed down, taught, and instructed from generation to generation, as Christ commanded.

Second, the church in Acts 2 devoted itself to the bread-breaking fellowship. The common way to translate this section between the two "ands" is "to fellowship, to the breaking of bread" to separate the two ideas. At the heart of the word *fellowship* is the idea of a communion, a common state of being.[16] A Christian is never more united to his brothers and sisters than when he is receiving Christ's body and blood with them in fellowship at the communion rail. Paul writes, "The cup

16 In his book *Echo: Unbroken Truth Worth Repeating Again*, Jonathan Fisk has an insightful discussion about the background of the word ***fellowship*** on pages 185–90. Boiled down, he suggests that instead of ***fellowship***, the word would be better understood as *fellowshape*.

of blessing that we bless, is it not a participation in the blood of Christ? The bread that we break, is it not a participation in the body of Christ?" (1 Corinthians 10:16). Both Luke in Acts 2:42 and Paul in 1 Corinthians 10:16 use the same Greek word, which is translated in English to "fellowship." This "participation," "communion," "common state of being" is found not over sharing the same hot dish or casserole or doing some other activity, which many American churches now envision as fellowship. Rather, fellowship is being united as brothers and sisters in the Meal Jesus gave to receive in remembrance of Him. Christ shapes us into His image, unites us with Him so that we have fellowship, communion, with Him and with one another as we gather together to break "bread"—that is, the "bread of life" (John 6:35).

And finally, the church in Acts 2 devoted itself to prayer. This was not simply saying a bunch of heartfelt extemporaneous prayers, as we imagine them to be today. "Prayer" refers to the Jewish liturgical prayers that were said throughout the day and at specific days in the year. These were written and memorized psalms and prayers said together in the temple and synagogues. This pattern of the prayers is the basis of the Christian liturgy used in many churches throughout time and the world.

Thus the church devoted itself to doctrine, Holy Baptism, the Sacrament of the Altar, and liturgy as it lived out Christ's exhortation: "Teaching them to guard all things whatsoever I have decreed to you" (Mark 13:23 Voth). The disciples were unified in this mission work. Two verses later, Luke records that the believers were "in the same and they had all things in common" (Acts 2:44 Voth). There are echoes here of Jesus' farewell discourse to teach and treasure "all things whatsoever." The church took Christ's exhortation to heart. All His decrees, commands, promises, and teachings are held in common and are the foundation of their fellowship around Him. The divisions we see in the Christian Church today didn't exist. Acts 4:32 says, "Now the full number of those who believed were of one heart and soul." They believed the same thing and were in the same understanding. They were united in doctrine, which was lived out together. The words *common* and *fellowship* share the same root word in Greek. There was a commonality, a unity, in their beliefs and their practice.

We see Paul encourage this same unity too. As the church grew, "having gone out" to various locations, we learn from Paul's epistles and from history that divisions, strifes, and schisms had entered into the church. These divisions were not mentioned in the beginning chapters of Acts. Paul wrote to the Christians in Corinth,

> I appeal to you, brothers, by the name of our Lord Jesus Christ, that all of you agree, and that there be no divisions among you, but that you be united in the same mind and the same judgment. (1 Corinthians 1:10)

Paul's urging that the church have the same view, mind, and purpose—unity in the teachings, or doctrines, of Christ and

His apostles—culminates in the discussion of the Lord's Supper and liturgical practices.

Jesus laid out very clearly in His farewell discourse how His church would grow. The church is to baptize and teach in the name of the triune God, and teach that all of Christ's words and actions, the entirety of the Holy Scriptures, is the authority of the church and the most prized, treasured possession a person can own.

By this baptizing and teaching, Christ will make disciples. He will create beloved brothers and sisters, children of His heavenly Father, who will abide in His Word and have eternal life. His plan for the church will endure in this earthly world until He comes to take His Bride home to the age that is to come—an age that will have no end. Until then, His church baptizes and teaches according to His command and promise in this age, which leads us into the second section of Matthew 28:20.

DISCUSSION QUESTIONS

1. How does the analogy of physical birth, eating, and nutrition relate to spiritual birth and growth?

2. What warning does Paul give in relation to false teachings? Why is it important to daily consume God's Word?

3. What does it mean to "guard all things" that Jesus has given to His church?

4. Why might pastors refrain from using personal stories in sermons?

5. What three activities did the early church devote itself to according to Acts 2:42–44?

6. How is the threefold enactment of Christ's command to be carried out in the local congregation today?

7. There are many ideas about how a church should grow in our world. What is the biblical teaching on church growth?

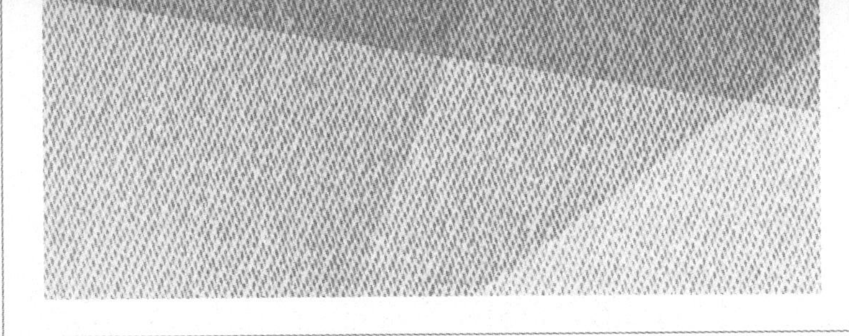

CHAPTER 8

MATTHEW 28:20B

And behold, I am with you always,
to the end of the age.

Jesus concluded His discourse with His disciples with these words. Matthew does not record any more words from Jesus, nor His ascension. These final words are the final promise from Christ to His church. "I am with you always." Let's take a closer look:

20"And behold,
I am with you all the days
until the fulfillment of the age."

(Voth)

When we looked at the context of Jesus' farewell discourse in chapter 1, we turned to the beginning of Matthew's Gospel account to the announcement of Jesus' birth to Joseph. In that announcement, the angel told Joseph that this child was going to be "'Immanuel' (which means, God with us)" (v. 23). Here we see that same language from Jesus Himself: "I am with you."

Christ with Us

One way to understand this statement is to see that Matthew has placed bookends around his Gospel account with Christ's words. Just as God took on human flesh in the incarnation by the Holy Spirit in the virgin Mary to become Immanuel, God is with us in the flesh now and continues as God and man with us. This is one of the attributes of God that Christ has. We use the term *omnipresent* to convey the truth that God is present everywhere. The Scripture verse, which is a source for this attribute, is from the prophet Jeremiah: "Can a man hide himself in secret places so that I cannot see him? declares the LORD. Do I not fill heaven and earth? declares the LORD" (23:24).

This is obviously a very good verse to see that God is indeed omnipresent, everywhere at all times—in heaven and on earth. There is no place we are that God isn't. For some, this is a scary thought, because it means that God knows all the sins we think we are hiding. But this should be a comforting thought, because we are never apart from God's gracious care and provision.

A second way to understand this promise, and perhaps how most Christians view it, is to spiritualize Christ's presence. In Acts 1, we read that Jesus ascended to His Father in heaven. His disciples no longer physically saw Jesus walking and talking with them. So when we read that Jesus has promised to be with us always but we don't see Him physically, we reason that He is with us in some other, nonphysical, unseen way. This sort of thinking can be found in the song "He Lives" by Alfred H.

Ackley. The last line of the first stanza speaks of knowing that Jesus lives because He is living in our heart.

The assurance of Christ's continued presence in this song is not the objective truth of the Holy Scriptures; it is instead the fickle feelings of our heart. Christ's presence is considered to be a mystical, spiritual presence that we cannot see but can experience, that we can feel in our hearts. Such heart-based feelings can be dangerous because they come and go and change constantly. Christ also warns that we cannot always trust our feelings because we remain sinner and saint: "For out of the heart come evil thoughts, murder, adultery, sexual immorality, theft, false witness, slander" (Matthew 15:19). To be fair, Paul says "that according to the riches of His glory He may grant you to be strengthened with power through His Spirit in your inner being, so that Christ may dwell in your hearts through faith" (Ephesians 3:16–17). We are given the gift of the Holy Spirit in the water and Word of Holy Baptism. Therefore, Christ dwells in our hearts. Yet knowing Christ because we feel some heartburn is not the same as the objective truth of having Christ revealed in the Holy Scriptures.

To understand Jesus being with us as a spiritual, warm, fuzzy feeling does not fit with the rest of His final discourse. Baptizing and teaching are not intellectual or mystical exercises of symbolism; they are concrete, objective realities conveyed in real ways.

Jesus knew He was returning to His Father in heaven. He spoke about it often, especially in the Upper Room on the night

He instituted His Supper. John records more of that conversation than any of the other Gospel accounts. It occupies chapters 13–17 of his Gospel. In chapter 14, John recounts the conversation about Christ's ascension and records these words:

> In My Father's house are many rooms. If it were not so, would I have told you that I go to prepare a place for you? And if I go and prepare a place for you, I will come again and will take you to Myself, that where I am you may be also. . . .
>
> I will not leave you as orphans; I will come to you. Yet a little while and the world will see Me no more, but you will see Me. Because I live, you also will live. (John 14:2–3, 18–19)

Jesus said He was leaving to go to His Father to prepare a place for His disciples, but He would not leave us alone, for He Himself will come to us, and we will see Him when He does. The last verse of Matthew is Jesus saying, "I am with you always" (28:20). Jesus left earth physically, yet He is with us always. He left earth, but He comes to us. We can't see Him, but we can. How can this be?

There are two places in Matthew where Jesus says He is with us. The first is Matthew 17, when the father of a demon-possessed son comes to Jesus explaining that the disciples were not able to heal the boy. Jesus, exasperated, says, "O faithless and twisted generation, how long am I to be with you? How long am I to bear with you? Bring him here to Me" (v. 17). Here, we see that Jesus was instructing the people, especially the disciples, that He would not be with them much longer in the same way He had been with them. In other words, Christ was pointing forward to His crucifixion and ascension.

Christ with Us in His Meal

In Matthew's Gospel, Jesus speaks about being "with you" in the Upper Room:

> Now as they were eating, Jesus took bread, and after blessing it broke it and gave it to the disciples, and said, "Take, eat; this is My body." And He took a cup, and when He had given thanks He gave it to them, saying, "Drink of it, all of you, for this is My blood of the covenant, which is poured out for many for the forgiveness of sins. I tell you I will not drink again of this fruit of the vine until that day when I drink it new *with you* in My Father's kingdom." (Matthew 26:26–29, emphasis added)

Christ's "with you" this time is in the context of His Holy Meal, the eating of His body and the drinking of His blood according to His command and institution postresurrection, when the Father's kingdom was inaugurated. "And even Christ's *promise* to be with His disciples is an echo of the promise made to Joshua by both Moses and God Himself that the Lord would be with him forever (Deuteronomy 31:8, 23; cf. Joshua 1:5). The covenant promise of God among His people in the Old

Testament becomes the promised presence of Jesus among His disciples."[17]

The new covenant in His blood, that is, the Lord's Supper, is how Christ is "with you" always. As God was with His people of old in a physical pillar of fire and a cloud of smoke, as He was present with His people in the thick darkness that dwelt above the atonement seat of the ark of the covenant in the Most Holy Place of the tabernacle, so Christ is present with you now as He tabernacles in the bread and wine, according to His institution and promise.

This is not a spiritual "with you" in your feelings but a real, concrete "with you" in the bread, which is His body, and in the wine, which is His blood. Truly, really present. Much ink has been spilled over how these words should be interpreted and how the Christian Church should celebrate the Lord's Supper. Here I spill a little more ink that will further the understanding that Christ is with us always.

Incarnation and the Real, Sacramental Presence

In the sixth month of Elizabeth's pregnancy, God sent an announcement to Mary through the words of an angelic messenger: "You will conceive in your womb and bear a son, and you shall call His name Jesus" (Luke 1:31). This was indeed startling news. Mary was a virgin, and virgins don't conceive and give birth to children. Gabriel assured Mary that this miracle would be fulfilled by the Holy Spirit, the power of the Most

17 Christopher J. H. Wright, *The Mission of God: Unlocking the Bible's Grand Narrative.* (IVP Academic, 2006), 355. Emphasis in original.

High, who would come upon and overshadow her, a human being. By the power of God's Word spoken through His messenger, Jesus became truly present in Mary's womb. Mary believed the Word of God that the messenger spoke to her: "Let it be to me according to your word" (v. 38). She did not participate in this event. She simply received the gift given by God's words and promises by faith.

To quickly and visually recap the incarnation of Christ, we will chart the events in this fashion:

LUKE 1:26–38		
Gabriel	messenger sent by God	
a son	message sent by God	
Mary's body	spoken over a physical element	
Jesus	now present	
no	seen with the eye	
faith	assurance that it's true	
none	human involvement	
"Let it be to me according to your word"	human response	

As the Christian Church carries out Christ's command to "do this in remembrance of Me" (1 Corinthians 11:24) in the Lord's Supper, the story of the incarnation is repeated in much the same way. God sends His messengers, pastors, to the church to proclaim His message, in this case the *verba* or Words of Institution as recorded by Matthew, Mark, Luke, and Paul. The physical elements of bread and wine are present before the messenger.

The question has been asked as to what is present once the messenger speaks Christ's Words of Institution. Some church bodies teach that the bread and wine are no more and literally become Christ's body and blood. Others teach that the bread and wine are still there, but Christ cannot be truly present for a variety of reasons: He has ascended to heaven, the finite cannot contain the infinite, the bread and wine are mere symbols, and so on. It is wise to let the mystery of Christ's words stand as they are recorded in Scripture. Christ's body is there in the bread, and His blood is there in the wine, just as His words say. Just as Mary could not explain how one moment she was not pregnant and then, according to God's Word, the Messiah was physically in her womb, we don't try to explain how God puts the body and blood of Jesus into or with the bread and wine. It is the mystery of God's ways that are above our ways. Faith simply takes God at His Word and believes it.

As the messenger—the pastor—speaks the message over physical elements, Christ Jesus becomes truly present. Can you see Jesus in the bread and wine with your physical eye? Of course not. But faith clings to the words and promises of God that says, "This is My body," "This is My blood," with bread and wine in His hand. Again, this is God's doing. It is not some special power entrusted to the messenger. It is God the Son fulfilling His Word of promise that the bread is His body and the wine is His blood. Our faithful response is not to question how or to reason it out, but to simply say, "Amen," that is, "Let it be to me according to your word" (Luke 1:38). The completed chart looks like this:

LUKE 1:26–38		LORD'S SUPPER
Gabriel	messenger sent by God	pastor
a son	message sent by God	*verba*
Mary's body	spoken over a physical element	bread and wine
Jesus	now present	Jesus
no	seen with the eye	no
faith	assurance that it's true	faith
none	human involvement	none
"Let it be to me according to your word"	human response	Amen

To recap: According to Christ's command and promise, He is present in the bread and wine; His very body and blood is in the Lord's Supper in the same way He was present at His incarnation in the virgin Mary. Because Jesus Himself declares the real presence, it is difficult to comprehend that some confess that He "was conceived by the Holy Spirit, born of the virgin Mary" but is not actually present in His Sacrament. If a virgin can become pregnant by God and God can become flesh and blood in her womb, then God certainly is present physically in bread and wine during Communion.

In the Lord's Supper, then, Jesus is with His church all the days of this age. Again, this is not just a spiritual presence but a body and blood presence that is just as real as when He was walking with His disciples. Christ intended for His church to eat of His body and drink of His blood to remember that He is with us always in this age. He has not abandoned us, leaving us as orphans. Rather, He remains with us in a very real way as His church gathers around Him. He has promised that we will see Him with the eyes of faith and truly see Him in bread and wine on the altars of our churches. "The Lord's Supper, which Christ instituted on the night that he was betrayed, is a meal for this time between the times."[18]

For This Time

Before we could stream and binge-watch several seasons of a favorite television show, it was frustrating when an episode concluded with "To be continued." We would have to wait a whole week, seven agonizing days, until the next episode would air. When a season ended, we would wait three or four months for the storyline to pick up. The show left us hanging, wondering what would happen next.

---

18 Gibbs, *Matthew 21:1–28:20*, 1413.

The Gospels have an element of "To be continued," but we know what will happen next. The Word of God delivers a promise that what Jesus and His church do now is what Jesus and His church will do forever.

"Time between times" brings us at last to the last words: "The fulfillment of the age" (Matthew 28:20 Voth). As I have stated, Christ remains with us in His Holy Supper. Paul writes, "For as often as you eat this bread and drink the cup, you proclaim the Lord's death until He comes" (1 Corinthians 11:26). The church celebrates the Lord's Supper and proclaims that Jesus is present in the bread and wine. It also proclaims that one day Jesus will come again. Christ has promised that He will return visibly to bring this age to an end, to its fulfillment, and bring us to the next age. There is a time coming when this age will cease and eternity will begin. And there the feast Jesus instituted for us will continue forever. Through His servant Isaiah, God promised,

> On this mountain the Lord of hosts will make for all peoples
> a feast of rich food, a feast of well-aged wine,
> of rich food full of marrow, of aged wine well refined.
> And He will swallow up on this mountain
> the covering that is cast over all peoples,
> the veil that is spread over all nations.
> He will swallow up death forever;

> and the Lord God will wipe away tears from all
> faces,
> and the reproach of His people He will take
> away from all the earth.
>
> (Isaiah 25:6–8)

Paul wrote, "But when the fullness of time had come, God sent forth His Son, born of woman, born under the law" (Galatians 4:4). In the same way that the time came for Christ to be born of Mary, the time will come for Christ to return "in His glory, and all the angels with Him, then He will sit on His glorious throne. Before Him will be gathered all the nations, and He will separate people one from another as a shepherd separates the sheep from the goats" (Matthew 25:31–32). At that time, this age will be fulfilled, completed, and ended so that the next age, the "life of the world to come" as we confess in the Nicene Creed, will begin.

Luther, too, points us to the connection of Christ with us in the Lord's Supper and the time between times.

> This then is what we call the correct use of the sacrament. It is not a matter of mere performance and of rendering obedience to the church, for even a pig might go to the sacrament in this way. It is not to be done for the sake of a good work, but in order that your heart should be strengthened, as the words say: "Which is given for you, which is poured out for you." And even if the words were

> not there, as when Paul omits them [1 Cor. 11:25], you still have the body which died for your sins and the blood which was poured out for them. But when Christ is given to you, forgiveness of sins is also given to you, and all that is procured through the treasure. . . . "This is the only treasure, the only forgiveness, and there is no other in heaven or on earth."
>
> For this reason Christ has given himself to us completely, and wishes to be and remain with us until the day of judgment [Matt. 28:20].[19]

Through the Lord's Supper, Christ is really, truly, actually present with His church all the days between His ascension and His return. The Christian Church's omission of this great promise by making it some sort of ethereal "Jesus is with me in my heart but not truly present with me" is a great loss. In Christ's farewell discourse, He points us to the place where He is found: on the altar in the bread and wine, just as He said, with our eyes set on the foretaste of the feast that is to come.

19 Martin Luther, *Luther's Works*, vol. 36, *Word and Sacrament II*, ed. Abdel Ross Wentz and Helmut T. Lehmann (Fortress Press, 1959), 350, 351.

DISCUSSION QUESTIONS

1. What dangers exist regarding a mystical, heart-based, feelings approach to Christ's presence with us always?

2. What concrete realities are conveyed through Baptism and teaching?

3. What is the Old Testament connection to Christ's abiding presence with us today?

4. What connections exist between Christ's incarnation and Christ's abiding presence with us in the Sacrament of the Altar?

5. What are the connections between the phrase "To be continued" and the way Jesus concluded His farewell discourse?

6. What is the significance of the Lord's Supper in relation to Jesus' promise to return?

7. What is the purpose of the Sacrament? How does it strengthen one's heart?

Conclusion

By inspiration of the Holy Spirit, Matthew records only one conversation between Jesus and His disciples after His resurrection from the dead. Matthew closes his Gospel with these words:

> 16The eleven disciples journeyed into Galilee
> to the mountain which Jesus
> designated to them,
> 17and having seen Him,
> they worshiped,
> but some doubted,
> 18and having drawn near,
> Jesus spoke to them, saying,
> "To Me has been given all authority
> in heaven and
> upon the earth.
> 19Therefore, having gone out,
> disciple all the Gentiles,
> baptizing them
> in the name of the Father and
> of the Son and
> of the Holy Spirit,

[20]teaching them
to guard all things whatsoever
I have decreed to you,
and behold,
I am with you all the days
until the fulfillment of the age."

(Voth)

This farewell discourse is about more than "You have to tell people about Jesus or they end up in hell on account of your silence." This is about Christ establishing His church, which Satan cannot prevail against. It is not full of legalistic commands that must be obeyed. It is full of Gospel, full of the Good News that Jesus has come to forgive sin, and this is news worth sharing. In our times, when so much of the world doubts the truth of the Scriptures, Jesus comes with the promise of forgiveness delivered to sinners in the teaching and preaching of Him and His Sacraments.

This deeper, better understanding of Jesus' farewell discourse as more than a legalistic command to tell others about Him begins in the Divine Service, in which Christ gives the church His gifts, namely the office of the holy ministry, to administer His gifts of Holy Absolution, Holy Baptism, teaching, and the Sacrament of the Altar.

Jesus comes with all the authority of His heavenly Father to forgive sin through His called ministers with the promise that all our sins are forgiven in heaven and on earth—which leaves no place where they are not forgiven. From this comes the direction and purpose for the Christian Church on earth:

- The church is to baptize all nations, young and old, every race, tribe, ethnicity. Differences in region, culture, or nationality do not matter. What matters is the church listening to the command of her Bridegroom, her Head, who instructs us to baptize, to apply water in any amount with His Word in the name of the triune God.
- The church is to teach Christ crucified to all who are gathered by God so that they may hold Him and His Word as their most prized possession.
- The church is to receive together His body and His blood in bread and wine in accordance with His Word so that what He won for us on the cross is delivered into us, through our mouths, sealing the doors of our body in the blood of the Lamb. In this way, He is always with us and always present as we are gathered around Him to receive His gifts.

Nothing New to See Here

The pattern we observe at the end of Matthew's Gospel is not the first time Matthew laid this out for us. When we look at the events of Jesus' life as Matthew recorded them, we find this same teaching in Matthew 9. In chapter 3 of this book, we looked briefly at the beginning of Matthew 9 when Jesus drew on His authority to forgive the sins of the man who was paralyzed. Jesus first forgave the man's sins. Then He healed him physically.

As Jesus left the house, He encountered Matthew sitting at the tax collector's booth. Jesus called out to him, "'Follow Me.' And he rose and followed Him" (Matthew 9:9). We see the phrase "following Jesus" in resurrection language connected with Holy Baptism in Paul's letter to the church in Rome:

> Do you not know that all of us who have been baptized into Christ Jesus were baptized into His death? We were buried therefore with Him by baptism into death, in order that, just as Christ was raised from the dead by the glory of the Father, we too might walk in newness of life.
>
> For if we have been united with Him in a death like His, we shall certainly be united with Him in a resurrection like His. (Romans 6:3–5)

The call to follow Jesus includes going to the cross with Jesus, dying with Jesus, being buried with Jesus, and resurrecting with Jesus. This is the language of Holy Baptism according to the Scriptures. Jesus called Matthew to follow Him into the waters of Holy Baptism to be crucified, buried, and to arise with Him in that Sacrament. Jesus absolved the man who was paralyzed and then baptized Matthew. Next, they ate a meal together, which, as you have read here, is the order of the farewell discourse.

Having absolved our sins, Jesus brought us into the waters of Holy Baptism, where we are united to Him in His death, burial, and resurrection. Then it is time for the party to start, and every good party includes food. Not just any food, but the real food that is His body and the real drink that is His blood. So we gather together, "tax collectors and sinners" (Matthew 9:10), to eat with Jesus, to eat of His body and drink His blood as He bids us do.

The Life of Christ's Church

This is the pattern of Christ's life. This is the pattern of the church's life in Christ. We confess that we cannot by our own reason or strength choose to believe in Jesus Christ as our Lord or come to Him by our own power. By the Holy Spirit, Christ calls us to gather around Him in the place He has promised to be that He might distribute His gifts to us. They come in simple ways through simple earthly things—water, voice, bread, and wine. But that doesn't make them something less. God has always elevated the simple things by His Word, including mankind by taking on our nature and form in His Son, our Lord Jesus Christ. In His farewell discourse, Christ gave gifts to His church and promised that He would build His church through these gifts—Holy Absolution, Holy Baptism, the Word of God, and the Holy Supper. When we ignore or neglect His gifts, we suffer. When we listen to His Word, when His gifts are rightly administered and proclaimed, His church remains faithful to her Bridegroom. Lord, grant that to us all!

By now you can see that there are many omissions from the way American Christianity has presented the Great Commission in the last two hundred years. Let us recover the true message of Jesus' farewell discourse and see how the Sacraments are at the center of the life of the church and the life of the Christian. Be gathered at the place that Jesus has designated for you to meet Him. Come worship Him and receive the gifts He gives you through His church: Holy Absolution, Holy Baptism, His Holy Word, and the Holy Supper.

In the name of Jesus. Amen.

DISCUSSION QUESTIONS

1. What is the main focus of Jesus' farewell discourse? How is this similar to and different from American Christianity's focus regarding the Great Commission?

2. What is the nature of Christ's church? In other words, what should she be busy doing according to Christ's farewell discourse?

3. What are the gifts Christ gave His church?

4. Why is it important to conform our ways to Christ's instructions?

5. What connections exist between Matthew 9 and 28?

6. What simple earthly things does Christ use to distribute His gifts?

7. How has this discussion of the omissions from the Great Commission in Jesus' farewell discourse furthered your understanding of the role of Jesus' life, death, and resurrection?

LEADER GUIDE

Dear leaders,

We have become so accustomed to hearing the term *the Great Commission* and the implications American Christianity has drawn from it that it may be difficult for some to accept a new—yet old—understanding of our Lord Jesus' final words to His disciples and the church. Be patient and let the Word of God accomplish the purpose for which it was sent. I am certain that this is not the final word on these verses but a discussion that will enable us to see the fullness of Christ and His gifts to us.

I also want to encourage you to keep the dialogue going. As we wrestle with the Word of God, we grow in thankfulness for all that God has done for us in Christ Jesus.

Finally, thank you for taking time to lead your brothers and sisters in this study of God's Word. I pray that it will strengthen the faith of all who participate as they receive the gifts that God gives them in His Word.

In Christ,

The author

Introduction

1. **What assumptions about the Great Commission are generally held by the Christian Church, particularly in the United States?**

   The words of the Great Commission are the marching orders or mission statements that every Christian must obey in much of American Christianity. There is an underlying assumption that Christians must evangelize to everyone they meet. If they do not, non-Christians will go to hell, and those who did not tell everyone they met about Jesus will be at fault. Another assumption is that the church will cease to exist or lose the role it once had in American culture if Christians do not obey the Great Commission.

2. **How do these assumptions line up with what you have heard preached and taught in your church?**

   Answers will vary based on each individual's past experiences.

3. **What are the consequences of these assumptions?**

   There has been a major shift in a majority of American churches. The focus has shifted away from building up one another in love and strengthening the faith of believers through solid preaching and teaching on Sunday mornings to recruiting people who do not believe. Anything associated with the historic church has been abandoned in an effort to not offend those who have no connection to it.

4. **How do comments like "God has called us to be great" make you feel about your own walk as a Christian?**

   Answers will vary, but when most Christians are asked about their walk as Christians, they do not describe it as being "great." Thus, statements like this can cause despair and feelings of failure.

5. **What changes have you observed in your church or the church in general based on this call to obey the Great Commission?**

   Answers will vary based on each individual's past experiences.

6. **What was the focus of the traditional understanding of Matthew 28:16–20 in the church?**

   The traditional understanding of Matthew 28:16–20 focused on the instructions from Jesus on how the church is to baptize and be united with Christ in the Sacrament of the Altar.

Chapter 1

1. **What is proof texting? How have you seen passages of Scripture taken out of context simply to prove someone's false belief?**

   Proof texting is taking a passage of Scripture out of its context to prove a point. Answers to the second question will vary based on each individual's past experiences.

2. **Why does the proper context matter when studying the Bible?**

   We must let each verse stand in its proper context to avoid proof texting and misunderstanding of a passage. False belief can be introduced when context is ignored. It also does not allow God's Word and will to be clearly communicated to the reader.

3. **Why do we let clear passages of Scripture inform the less clear passages?**

   This, again, prevents false belief and doubt and helps further our understanding of Scripture.

4. **Describe how the inverted triangle (see p. 21) is a helpful tool for proper biblical interpretation.**

   The inverted triangle gives readers a framework to move from the larger context of a passage to a narrowed view and a right understanding of the passage(s) being discussed.

5. **What boundaries did Jesus set for the disciples' first preaching expedition? How does this differ from what you know and understand about the Great Commission?**

   Matthew 10 records that Jesus set the boundary for the disciples to drive out demons and heal the sick. Their mission was limited in scope of activity and place. Answers to the second question will vary. The second question is intended to let readers know that Jesus sets boundaries to

His promises, which may not require us to go overseas for missions, for example.

6. **God's command in Deuteronomy 7 may look harsh and uncharacteristic of God at first, but it is there to protect God's people from actions that will destroy them and their faith. How do the Commandments do the same thing for us today?**

   The Ten Commandments are not given by God to rob us of joy but to protect us from thoughts, words, and deeds that would hurt us. Disregard for authorities can lead to incarceration. Speaking ill of another person violates the Eighth Commandment and creates a barrier to loving others as we have been loved. Desiring our neighbor's wife can lead to adultery, destroying what God has joined together.

7. **How does biblical geography help us understand another level of context of the passage?**

   The physical location of a biblical event helps clarify the lesson of the event. Jesus said and did things differently in Gentile regions than He did in Jewish regions. Matthew 28 records that Galilee was surrounded by Gentile lands, many of which were visible from a mountaintop. The disciples could literally see where they would be going to proclaim the Gospel.

Chapter 2

1. **What benefits come from a more literal translation that ignores standard English grammatical rules?**

   A more literal translation forces you to slow down, hear a passage in a new way, and see the connections that might otherwise go unseen.

2. **Today we speak of "mountaintop experiences" as times of great personal spiritual highs. How does that differ from biblical mountain encounters with God?**

   Biblical mountaintop experiences were times when God met with His people to give them His gifts. The focus of those experiences was always on God's actions for us, not our feelings.

3. **What is a theophany? Where do we see theophanies in the Scriptures?**

   A theophany is a visible appearance of God to men. A few examples include God appearing to Moses in the burning bush on Mount Sinai, God appearing to the Israelites in the pillar of fire and pillar of cloud after their exodus from Egypt, the Lord speaking to Elijah in a low whisper, and Jesus' transfiguration.

4. **What common theme is seen in all the mountain encounters mentioned? What role did the preincarnate/incarnate Jesus play in these encounters?**

God came to His people during these mountain encounters to give them a gift—be it commands to protect them or assurance that they were not alone in the faith. Jesus, as the Word of God, came to His people in bodily form (e.g., Joshua saw and heard the Angel of the Lord, as recorded in Joshua 5:13–6:7).

5. **What pattern of divine service do we see in these mountaintop accounts? What does this pattern teach us about our daily life?**

   Jesus is the one who comes to His people in the Old and New Testaments to give them gifts at the place He designates. We do not determine where we will meet God. Jesus has not promised to come to the local country club to hand out His gifts. We are gathered by the Holy Spirit at the place Jesus promises to meet us.

6. **What is the significance of these verses, which were the last words Jesus spoke to His disciples before His ascension?**

   Jesus was preparing to depart from His disciples. He left them with His parting gifts so that they would be comforted when they could no longer see Him.

7. **When was the last time you heard this verse discussed as part of the Great Commission? What insight does it bring to the understanding of these verses?**

Answers will vary based on each individual's past experiences. When we read these verses in their proper context, the Great Commission should be read as a comforting and reassuring message from Jesus rather than a command that can lead to despair.

Chapter 3

1. **What is the difference between the modern American understanding of worship and what the Bible teaches about the Divine Service?**

   Much of American Christianity is focused on doing something for God, even in worship. But the Divine Service is where the triune God does something for us in that He comes to give us forgiveness, life, and salvation. This is comforting to a conscience troubled by sin and surrounded by death and destruction.

2. **What did God give the children of Israel when they arrived at Mount Sinai?**

   He gave the Ten Commandments and all things necessary for His continued presence with them, such as the tabernacle and the sacrificial system.

3. **What are some of the gifts the triune God gives us during the Divine Service?**

   He gives Holy Baptism, by which we enter into the church, declaring His name upon us and giving us forgiveness of our sins. We sing "with angels and archangels and with all the company of heaven," (*LSB*, p. 208) a joyous comfort to those whose loved ones have departed in faith. We hear God's Word proclaimed to us. We bring our petitions before Him, knowing that He answers our every prayer according to His good and gracious will. We receive the gift of Jesus' body and blood for our forgiveness and salvation.

4. **How are the disciples described in the Gospel accounts, especially after Jesus' resurrection?**

   The disciples were very real people who sinned like we do. They had moments of great faith and times of poverty of faith. They heard Jesus' words of instruction and forgiveness and received His gifts, just as we hear and receive them in the Divine Service. They repented of their sins and shared the Gospel message of grace, mercy, and forgiveness through their actions, just like we do.

5. **How does knowing that the disciples had doubts help you as a Christian?**

   Answers will vary but should include a discussion about their sinful human nature. We struggle day in and day out to overcome our sin and the temptations of the world, just like the disciples did.

6. **What is the significance of the father's statement, "I believe; help my unbelief!" (Mark 9:24)?**

   Doubt is not rank unbelief. We believe in Jesus as our Redeemer and Savior, but we have doubt that can be mis-understood as lack of faith or unbelief sometimes. Some accounts in the Bible are difficult for our mortal minds to grasp, including the fact that we are saved by Jesus' death. We believe this to be true, but sometimes we doubt because our own weakness and sinfulness is great. Lord, help us believe all that You have said and done!

7. **How do the dichotomies of doubt and worship, Law and Gospel, sinner and saint help you rightly understand your life as a Christian?**

   Christians live in a tension in this life that must be held in balance. God gathers us to the places He designates to give us gifts. We return thanks and praise, serve and obey Him. We need to be convicted of sin to hear the beauty of forgiveness in Christ. We are held in tension in this life as sinners. But because of Christ, we stand holy and innocent before the Father. When one aspect weighs more, we become unbalanced, given to pride or despair, trusting in ourselves rather than Christ.

Chapter 4

1. **Who initiated the conversation between Jesus and the disciples? What implication does this have in rightly understanding these verses and the Christian mission in general?**

   Jesus initiated the conversation. As a matter of fact, the disciples never spoke. The rhetoric of American Christianity is often about us finding Jesus or doing something for Him. Yet Scripture confirms that it is Jesus who begins all things and comes to us with His gifts. Even in mission work, it is Jesus who acts to bring faith and peace to troubled hearts.

2. **How does the account of the man who was paralyzed show Jesus' authority to forgive sins?**

   The scribes were right: No one has the power to forgive except God alone. What they failed to comprehend was that God was standing there in the flesh doing what He does: forgiving sins.

3. **Why did Jesus begin His discourse with comfort, assurance, peace, and the Gospel? Why did the disciples need to hear that Jesus had the authority to forgive their sins?**

   The last time the disciples had seen Jesus alive was when He was arrested at Gethsemane. They fled and abandoned Him when that happened. They had betrayed Him and were living in fear and regret. Jesus came to them not to condemn but to forgive them and comfort them with His peace. This authority to forgive sins lifted a burdened conscience into a state of comfort.

4. **How does Jesus' authority to forgive sins relate to the proclamation of the church?**

   If our sin is only forgiven on earth, then we still stand condemned before God in heaven. That would not be good news, and we would still be tormented by our sin. But Christ Jesus has given the church the authority to forgive sin on earth and in heaven. That is Good News—the Gospel—the proclamation of the church that we are forgiven by God in heaven and on earth.

5. **What connections exist between Matthew 16 and Matthew 28?**

   Jesus gave His disciples instructions regarding what they were to do, whom they were to go to, and the scope of their work in both chapters. Understanding Matthew 16 helps us see the expanded version of Matthew 28.

6. **Why is it important to communicate and deliver the forgiveness of sins to others?**

   We daily sin much and need to hear the assurance that our sins have been forgiven by Christ Jesus in His death on the cross.

7. **What is the comfort you receive in Holy Absolution from Christ via your pastor?**

   Answers may vary but should be connected to the assurance that Christ, through the pastor, has forgiven sin and granted His peace.

Chapter 5

1. **What are the differences in emphasis between the standard understanding of these verses as the Great Commission versus as a farewell discourse?**

   Chief among the differences is who the main actor is in carrying out what is to be accomplished. The standard understanding places all the emphasis on what Christians are to do for God. The farewell discourse affirms what God has done for us in Christ Jesus and our joyful response.

2. **What is the significance of using "having gone out" instead of "go"?**

   "Go" implies planning, leaving, and heading somewhere else. It can also imply big actions that are worthy of being posted on social media. "Having gone out" describes your daily interactions and intentionality to share Jesus with others.

3. **"Having gone out," where do you have the opportunity to make disciples?**

   Answers will vary based on each individual's experiences.

4. **How does the effect of the word *therefore* change when this verse is pulled out of its context? How does the word *therefore* change the motivation of the discourse when it is tied to Jesus' words in verse 18?**

   Therefore always implies an antecedent—that is, something beforehand that creates a cause-and-effect scenario. When verse 19 is pulled out of its context with verse 18, "go" becomes the antecedent for "therefore," and the motivation for telling people about Jesus is based in the Law. When "therefore" is seen in context with verse 18, Jesus receiving authority becomes the cause, and the motivation for "going" and "making disciples" shifts to the grace and forgiveness of the resurrected Jesus, which results in joyfully telling others what Jesus has done for us.

5. **What is the difference in the motivations for proclaiming the Gospel from the Great Commission understanding and proclaiming it from the farewell discourse view?**

   The difference cannot be stated enough. American Christianity's Great Commission understanding is based on the Law: You *must* do this. The farewell discourse places the motivation in the joyful response of the Christian, who has been forgiven in Christ's sacrificial death and given new life through His resurrection—a life grounded in His Word and Sacraments.

6. **What are the similarities and differences between Matthew 10 and Matthew 28?**

   Both chapters retell accounts of Jesus sending His disciples, but the "to whom" expands from Israel outward to the world. Chapter 10 includes preaching forgiveness, as does chapter 28. But Jesus commands preaching along with instruction of the Sacraments of Holy Baptism, Holy Absolution, and Holy Communion in the latter.

7. **If the Gospel is for Jews and Gentiles, who are we prohibited from sharing the Gospel with?**

   No one. We are to share the Good News of Jesus with everyone, especially our enemies.

Excursus

1. **How is "abide" used throughout John's Gospel?**

   John uses "abide" to be the place where Jesus is found.

2. **Where do you find Jesus abiding today?**

   Jesus abides in His Word and Sacraments in the Divine Service.

3. **What does Christ's abiding presence mean in your life?**

   Answers may vary, but the focus should be on the abiding presence of Christ in our lives as we are gathered in the Divine Service to receive His gifts to us.

4. **Compare and contrast "Go and make" and "Come and see." Which one is more freeing and joyous for you as a Christian?**

   Again, it's motivation by the Law, "You must go" and "You must make," versus an invitation to trust that God will accomplish His purpose as we invite people to come and see Jesus where He has promised to abide—in His Word and Sacraments—which is how He brings people to faith.

5. **How does the sequence of events at Jacob's well challenge the idea of meeting people where they are in missions?**

   The woman went to where Jesus was abiding. He began the conversation with her in order to save her. Then she told others about Jesus and invited them to come and see for themselves. Others then went to the place where Jesus was abiding and heard His words, which created faith.

6. **How did doubt play a role in the woman at the well's faith?**

   She had faith that Jesus is the Christ, but there was still doubt about what that meant for her life.

7. **The man who was paralyzed was brought by his friends to where Jesus was abiding. How does this relate to missions today?**

   The man was paralyzed, unable to bring himself to the place where Jesus was abiding. Sinful humans are dead, paralyzed, unable to bring themselves to the place where Jesus is abiding. They aren't even looking. As followers of Jesus, we are called to bring them to the place where Jesus is abiding so that He may change their hearts from unbelief to belief.

Chapter 6

1. **What is the basic meaning of the Greek word *baptizo*, which is transliterated in English as *baptize*?**

   To apply water, often in a religiously ceremonial way.

2. **What is the important part of Christian Baptism? The age it happens, the amount of water that is used, or fulfilling the command of Jesus? Why?**

   Fulfilling the command of Jesus is clearly the most important part. The age it happens, the amount of water that should be used, and so on are not specified in the Bible. What is specified is Jesus' command to baptize with water and in the name of the Father and of the Son and of the Holy Spirit.

3. **Why did Nicodemus misunderstand Jesus' statement about being "born from above"?**

   Words can be the same but have different meanings based on context, which is sometimes difficult to determine at first.

4. **Like Nicodemus's misunderstanding of Jesus' statement, what other examples can you think of that involve a play on words and meanings?**

   Answers will vary. Examples include *pair*, as in two, and *pear*, the fruit; *organ*, as in a musical instrument or as a part of the human body.

5. **What is the connection between earthly birth and heavenly birth?**

   Just as you had nothing to do with your earthly birth, you have nothing to do with your heavenly birth. Both are gifts of God apart from you and your actions.

6. **What historical event did Jesus use to draw a parallel between earthly and heavenly salvation? What is the connection to Jesus being lifted up?**

The parallel is made in the fiery serpent in the wilderness narrative in Numbers 21. When the children of Israel looked in faith at the lifted-up serpent, they were saved from the deadly poison. In a similar way, when we look in faith at the lifted-up Christ on the cross, we are saved from sin and death by the death and resurrection of Jesus.

7. **What is the connection between Holy Baptism and Jesus' crucifixion?**

   Holy Baptism is a heavenly birth gifted to us by God as He joins us to Jesus' death, burial, and resurrection.

Chapter 7

1. **How does the analogy of physical birth, eating, and nutrition relate to spiritual birth and growth?**

   Just as our physical bodies need proper nourishment, our faith must be fed with solid biblical preaching and teaching.

2. **What warning does Paul give in relation to false teachings? Why is it important to daily consume God's Word?**

   We are to avoid false teachings because they pander to the sinful nature of mankind. The best way to avoid them is to daily feast on God's Word so that we may recognize the truth of God and not be misled by the lies of the fallen world.

3. **What does it mean to "guard all things" that Jesus has given to His church?**

To guard is to treasure, to make it the most important thing in your life so that you will do anything to protect it—even give your life for it. "All" means everything, even those parts we do not like. Christ's gifts are for our present and eternal good, not harm, so we cherish them as the most important gifts we have ever received.

4. **Why might pastors refrain from using personal stories in their sermons?**

   We are commanded to preach Jesus Christ and Him crucified (see 1 Corinthians 1:23) at all times. The sermon is to be about Jesus, not the pastor. The pastor cannot preach what he likes or what he thinks to be right, but he is to preach the Gospel. The same goes for teaching. The pastor is to teach what Jesus has said, not what man invents, such as myths and fabricated stories.

5. **What three activities did the early church devote itself to according to Acts 2:42–44?**

   The teachings or doctrines of the apostles, the breaking of bread in Holy Communion, and the prayers.

6. **How is the threefold enactment of Christ's command to be carried out in the local congregation today?**

   The church, and especially the pastor, is not to change what Christ has gifted to us through His teachings, His Sacraments, and the Divine Service. We do as we have been commanded by Christ.

7. **There are many ideas about how a church should grow in our world. What is the biblical teaching on church growth?**

   Jesus protects and expands His church according to His promise. We do not grow the church. Rather, we bring people to the place where Jesus abides in His Word and Sacraments. God converts them, thus growing the church. We are called to be faithful.

Chapter 8

1. **What dangers exist regarding a mystical, heart-based, feelings approach to Christ's presence with us always?**

   Feelings ebb and flow. If you look to your feelings for assurance that Christ is with us, you might assume that Christ is absent when that feeling is absent.

2. **What concrete realities are conveyed through Baptism and teaching?**

   The objective truth of God's unbroken promises is declared in the Word and Sacraments. The Lord God is faithful and does not change, unlike our feelings and emotions. The unwavering, never-failing promise that Christ is with us in His Word and Sacraments is grounded in Baptism, Holy Communion, and the teachings of the Scriptures.

3. **What is the Old Testament connection to Christ's abiding presence with us today?**

In the Old Testament, God was with His people in the tabernacle (later the temple) between the wings of the cherubim in the Most Holy Place. Today, God is with His people in the body and blood tabernacle of Jesus in Holy Communion.

4. **What connections exist between Christ's incarnation and Christ's abiding presence with us in the Sacrament of the Altar?**

   There is a messenger sent by God, with His message to the hearer spoken over a physical element, whereby Jesus becomes truly present in both cases. We cannot see the baby Jesus in the womb or Jesus in the bread and wine, but we believe what God has said in His Word by faith. Our involvement is not in the action but in receiving the gift according to God's words and promises.

5. **What are the connections between the phrase "To be continued" and the way Jesus concluded His farewell discourse?**

   Jesus has returned to the Father's right hand, but He will come again. We are living in the "to be continued" time before He comes again physically and visibly in power and glory to judge the living and the dead. We are in the time between the ascension and the return of Christ.

6. **What is the significance of the Lord's Supper in relation to Jesus' promise to return?**

   As the church proclaims that Jesus is with us sacramentally in His Supper, we, as the church on earth, proclaim that one day He will be with us again just as He was with His disciples when He instituted His Supper.

7. **What is the purpose of the Sacrament? How does it strengthen one's heart?**

The purpose of the Sacrament is for Christ to be with His Bride, the church, always, so that all may be assured that their sins are forgiven and eternal life with Him awaits.

Conclusion

1. **What is the main focus of Jesus' farewell discourse? How is this similar to and different from American Christianity's focus regarding the Great Commission?**

This text is about Christ Jesus establishing His church through Word and Sacraments as gifts from the triune God to you. The traditional emphasis on spreading the Good News is here, but in a much more joyous manner that flows from the forgiveness of sins. The emphasis on conversion is properly grounded in the work of Christ, not in our actions or doings. Finally, the assurance that Jesus is with us always is grounded in the gift of the Sacrament of the Altar, not in how we happen to feel at the moment.

2. **What is the nature of Christ's church? In other words, what should she be busy doing according to Christ's farewell discourse?**

The church is to be busy absolving sinners, baptizing all nations, teaching Christ crucified in accordance with His

Word, and partaking of the body and blood of Jesus in the Holy Supper.

3. **What are the gifts Christ gave His church?**

   Christ has gifted His church the office of the holy ministry (pastors), Holy Absolution, Holy Baptism, teaching and preaching, and the Sacrament of the Altar.

4. **Why is it important to conform our ways to Christ's instructions?**

   Christ promises to sustain and grow His church according to His instructions, not ours. When we try to make our own way apart from His instructions, there is no promise to grow or even preserve the church.

5. **What connections exist between Matthew 9 and 28?**

   The pattern of forgiving, baptizing, teaching, and eating together are found in both chapters.

6. **What simple earthly things does Christ use to distribute His gifts?**

   Jesus uses the voice of the pastor to declare His forgiveness in Holy Absolution. Baptism brings forgiveness and the gift of the Holy Spirit through simple water and Christ's command. God comes to us with His words of Law and Gospel, including in words seen in a Bible or heard during sermons. Jesus promises His body and blood are present for the forgiveness of sins in the bread and wine during Holy

Communion. Voices, water, bread, and wine are all earthly things Christ uses to distribute His gifts to us.

7. **How has this discussion of the omissions from the Great Commission in Jesus' farewell discourse furthered your understanding of the role of Jesus' life, death, and resurrection?**

   Answers will vary based on each individual's experiences.